RHODESIA
The Story of the Crisis

RHODESIA
The Story of the Crisis

DESMOND LARDNER-BURKE

Foreword by
The Hon. IAN DOUGLAS SMITH

OLDBOURNE · LONDON

OLDBOURNE BOOK CO. LTD
1–5 PORTPOOL LANE, LONDON E.C.1

PRINTED AND BOUND IN GREAT BRITAIN BY PURNELL
AND SONS LTD, PAULTON (SOMERSET) AND LONDON

Contents

2nd August, 1966.

Having been closely associated with
Desmond Lardner Burke from that day in 1948
when we first entered the Rhodesia Parliament
as new and inexperienced back-benchers, I can
speak with some authority to the reputation he
possesses of being a direct and forthright
exponent of those things he believes to be for
the good of all the people of Rhodesia.

As a member of my Cabinet he has been a
participant in all the long and fruitless
negotiations that I have had with successive
British Governments and which culminated in the
assumption by Rhodesia of her democratic rights
on the 11th November last year.

He has now written his version of the
inside story of the last phase of the negotiations
which took place during the latter half of 1965,
and I think that the viewpoint he presents will
do much to silence the critics of Rhodesia who
claim intransigence on the part of my team of
negotiators.

I commend this book to all those who

would like to know more about those dramatic
days during which we, the people of Rhodesia ,
decided that we would no longer be party to the
decline and fall of the once great British Empire.

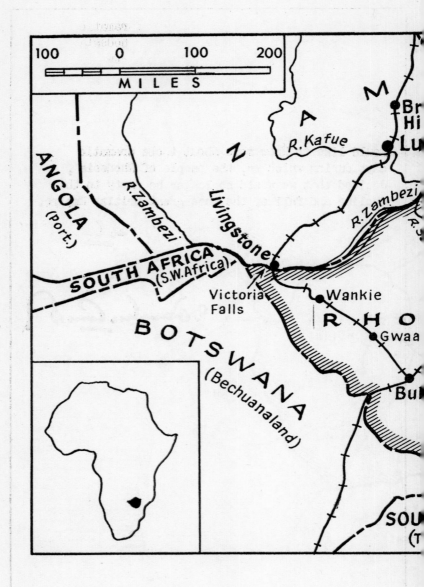

Author's Note

In writing this book I wish to make it perfectly clear that the contents do not necessarily express the views of the Rhodesian Government or any colleagues of mine in the Cabinet. This is entirely my personal impression gained during the discussions that took place. It should also be made clear that in writing these impressions it has been done merely to place on record how I view the discussions. It is not done in any way with a view to obtaining any recompense and any financial advantage that may occur from it will be passed on by me to some charity in Rhodesia.

1

Introduction

It is Rhodesia's legitimate pride that in seventy-six short years she has built up one of the most progressive nations in Africa from virtually nothing.

When the British Pioneer Column reached the place we now call Cecil Square on the 12th November 1890 the Mashonas, the inhabitants of the country, were being systematically raided and exterminated by the Matabele tribes. There was no security, no justice, no roads, sanitation or trade. Four hundred thousand Africans went in daily dread of massacre, their women in fear of captivity and rape.

Today, seventy-six years later, a great young nation has been built up. Over four million Africans live in security and peace. Parliament functions normally. The courts are admitted to be entirely independent and to administer justice without fear or favour to black and white Rhodesians alike; nearly four hundred thousand Africans from other states come to Rhodesia to work because wages are higher, the conditions of life safer and freer than in their own countries.

A large and dynamic economy has been built up by the development of a huge tobacco industry and by exploiting the immense mineral resources of the nation. And this has been accomplished between 1890 and 1966.

But all this was not achieved without the sweat and tears that go to make a nation. The early wars against the Matabele were soon forgotten. Rhodesia gave her treasure and her men to die in both world wars fighting alongside Britain. She survived the terrible economic slump of the thirties. Rhodesia began to expand in a big way.

After forty-three years of self-government, Rhodesia negotiated for her Independence in 1965, failed to achieve it by negotiation, and proclaimed it of her own volition and accord.

'We have struck a blow for the preservation of justice, civilization, and Christianity, and in the spirit of this belief we have this day assumed our sovereign independence. God bless you all.'

With these solemn words, Prime Minister Ian Douglas Smith, of Rhodesia, ended an historic broadcast on 11th November 1965. The nation – and indeed the whole world – now knew that Rhodesia no longer recognized any outside suzerainty; that a little country was prepared, if necessary, to defend its rightful heritage to its utmost ability.

The Prime Minister's historic broadcast marked the end of a twilight of uncertainty, doubt, and, at times, deep frustration. While Rhodesians steeled themselves to face up to whatever retribution other people might seek to visit upon them, they did so with a great surge of hope, determination – and relief.

All the equivocation, deceit and procrastination were now over. It was like coming out of a dark cave into the clean, free sunlight. They would – and if necessary they will – pay any price.

It was Prime Minister Smith who read the Declaration

of Independence. It was Prime Minister Harold Wilson and his colleagues who rendered this inevitable. They left Rhodesia no other choice.

The story really begins in 1923 – more than forty years ago – when Rhodesia became a self-governing Colony. From that date there was established an unblemished record of progress, stability, justice and orderly government. Standards already second to none on the continent of Africa were raised for all Rhodesians. Medical services, schools, railways, roads, churches, fine cities, housing, factories, technical and agricultural colleges – a university – all the things that go to make the modern progressive state: the proud legacy of forty-two years of self-rule. Rhodesia has her faults and has made mistakes. But on balance she is proud of her achievements.

When the Pioneers first arrived in the latter part of the last century, thrusting through malarial bush in ox wagons, they found a savage, untamed wilderness. Sickness, tribal war and slavery – along with incredibly primitive ignorance – were the lot of the comparative handful of tribesmen they encountered. The estimated African population of that time was at most 400,000. Because of the hospitals, doctors and nursing staff introduced by those first white Rhodesians, and the extension of civilization, the African population today has grown to nearly 4,000,000, of which 2,000,000 are children – a tribute in itself to the country's medical advance.

A state was established that became the envy of other countries in Africa. None could match Rhodesia's achievements in social services, economic expansion and constant, orderly government.

Throughout this whole period its citizens remained dedicated to the British way of life. They based everything on the principles of fair play, tolerance and opportunity for all, and they remained unswervingly loyal to Britain; their deep affection for the Crown remained unsurpassed.

In 1953 the now defunct Federation of Rhodesia and Nyasaland was established. Of the three territories involved, Rhodesia was the only one, by virtue of its self-ruling status, to put the matter squarely to the people in a referendum. The answer was 'Yes' and thenceforth Rhodesia put all her efforts into making a success of Federation. Economically, tremendous strides were made.

The story is well known that in 1963 the British Government rejected its own creation and, without the concurrence of either the Rhodesian Government or the over-all Federal Government, dissolved the Federation. Meanwhile, in 1961 the Rhodesian people accepted, by referendum, a new Constitution which conferred independence 'within the Federal framework'.

The 1961 Constitution was the result of round-table talks between all parties and all races, presided over by Britain's then Commonwealth Secretary, Mr Duncan Sandys. African Nationalists accepted it to a man . . . and within days repudiated it to a man. It is emphasized that, whatever may now be said, the 1961 Constitution was sold to Rhodesia as conferring independence subject to Federal ties.

When Britain unilaterally dissolved the Federation, it became apparent that in her eyes the independence Rhodesia had been granted 'within the Federal framework' had largely evaporated – but at the same time all the concessions and agreements Rhodesia had made to achieve this non-existent independence were still binding. In short, she had been misled into making extra-ordinarily generous concessions – for nothing.

While Rhodesia continued scrupulously to observe the 1961 Constitution in the belief that it was the basis for sovereign independence, the British Government was clearly determined to use the new situation as a means of swiftly promoting so-called majority rule.

It took two years of intensive negotiation, and finally something close to an ultimatum, to wring the truth of this assertion out of the British Government. The 1961 concessions were not enough. The 1961 Constitution was no longer considered a fair basis for Independence.

The fundamental difference between the Rhodesian and British Governments was this. Rhodesians believe that the reins of government should be held in respon-sible hands. The colour of those hands is immaterial. The majority of those capable of exercising a vote, and thus being responsible for government, are Europeans by virtue of their qualifying with the required standards. In time a greater proportion of the population will be-come eligible to vote and therefore exercise an increasing and, it is hoped, responsible influence. The British Government, on the other hand, believe in what they euphemistically term 'majority rule', by which they mean black rule, which is blatant racialism. The fact that in several previous exercises of this kind the 'one man, one vote' principle in Africa has led to one election, one party, one dictator – is apparently of no consequence.

When the London talks broke down in October 1965, the Prime Minister, Mr Ian Smith, told a Press Con-ference: 'The British Government has categorically stated that it no longer believes that the 1961 Constitu-tion is an appropriate basis for Independence. This is contrary to everything we have been led to believe in the past.'

This disclosure, flashed back from London to Rhodesia, was taken as a clear indication by most Rhodesians that the British Government was planning to double-cross Mr Smith, just as it had Sir Roy Welensky, the Federal Prime Minister.

During the talk, Mr Smith had offered the British Government his full acceptance of the principles of unimpeded progress towards majority rule as enshrined in the 1961 Constitution. He offered a means of providing the frequently referred to 'blocking third' against amendment of the entrenched clauses in the Constitution with an Upper House comprised of African Chiefs. As the first representative of a country which has honoured every guarantee and commitment it had ever entered into, he was prepared to offer guarantees ensuring that there would be no tampering with the Constitution.

But if Mr Smith failed to make headway with the British Government, he certainly succeeded with the British people. Expressions of sympathy and goodwill poured into Rhodesia House from all over the United Kingdom.

Back in Salisbury, Mr Smith received a further appeal from Mr Wilson; Rhodesia's Prime Minister responded with the offer of a solemn treaty guaranteeing the inviolability of the Constitution. Then came Mr Wilson's dramatic announcement that he would fly to Rhodesia.

Rhodesians began to ask themselves: 'Is he in earnest this time, at last? Surely he can't still be stalling . . . or can he?' He could! Mr Wilson and his Commonwealth Relations Secretary, Mr Arthur Bottomley, arrived with an impressive corps of fifty British civil servants.

Hopefully, Rhodesians began to wonder if this enormous retinue meant that, in addition to top-level talks, there would be liaison at all levels in the process of working out the complicated details of Independence.

Mr Wilson embarked on talks with individuals and organizations. Of those whom he chose or agreed to see, the majority had never received a single vote from the people of Rhodesia and were in no way representative of public opinion.

While the British Prime Minister gave only one hour of his time to the Council of Chiefs (the acknowledged leaders of 80 per cent of the African population) he gave nearly a full day to rival Nationalist delegations led by men who had either never fought an election or who had never had a vote of any sort cast in their favour.

Hope surged again in Rhodesia when it was announced that proposals for the establishment of a Royal Commission were to be considered by the two Governments. The Rhodesian Government was prepared to abide by the findings of such a Royal Commission, with the proviso that the Commission's terms of reference should be to find out whether or not Independence, on the existing Constitution appropriately amended to accord with the views of the Rhodesian Government, was acceptable to the majority of the people in Rhodesia.

It is probable that with goodwill on both sides – and this was certainly forthcoming from the Rhodesian side – the Commission could have evolved its own *modus operandi* which would have been acceptable to all parties. But on his return to London Mr Wilson had clearly done some rethinking . . .

In his statement to the House of Commons he hedged the proposal round with so many conditions that it

B

became hopeless. For example, he laid down how it should operate instead of leaving it to the Commission to make its own proposals in an interim report. He insisted that the Commission should make known throughout Rhodesia the British Government's opposition to the views of the Rhodesian Government, thus seeking to turn an intended impartial body into a propaganda vehicle.

He stated that unless the Commission's report was unanimous it would be unacceptable – and on top of all that he 'reserved the British Government's position at all stages'. In other words, had the Commission finally come forward with a unanimous report in favour of the Rhodesian Government, the British Government could still have rejected it.

Rhodesians felt that had Mr Wilson really been sincere about the Royal Commission proposal he would himself have stayed in Rhodesia to reach agreement on its terms of reference. Leaving Mr Bottomley behind for twenty-four hours, ostensibly for this purpose, was no more than a token gesture.

They now believe – and, reluctantly, so did the Rhodesian Government before it was driven to take the final step – that Mr Wilson's visit with his coterie of civil servants and the later arrival of the British Attorney-general, Sir Elwyn Jones, was a gigantic charade intended to convince the British electorate that 'I did everything humanly possible'. No compromise solution was really wanted.

2

The Dispute in Outline

The momentous decision to assume Independence, taken on 11th November 1965, was not reached by the elected leaders of Rhodesia without full and solemn consideration of all the circumstances. Every possible alternative was examined, every avenue of negotiation with successive British Governments fully explored, before the end of the verbal conflict with Britain was reached.

The consequences which were likely to follow in the wake of this decision were well known to the peoples of Rhodesia: they realized the implications of the step that had to be taken; they realized that the Independence which they now cherish would not be won without difficulty. But they were fortified in the knowledge that, in the final analysis, Rhodesia must avoid the path laid by British politicians in recent years, a path which would lead Rhodesia's security and prosperity into an insecure and negative future, and that they had no real alternative if they were to continue to protect the ideals of the free world and promote the interests of all Rhodesians, regardless of colour or creed.

For a fuller understanding of the reasons underlying Rhodesia's decision to cut the final and nebulous constitutional tie linking her to a Government isolated by some six thousand miles from the realities of the African scene, it is necessary to look briefly at Rhodesia's history.

Britain has never governed Rhodesia. Prior to 1923, the country had been administered under Royal Charter, by the British South Africa Company. Throughout Rhodesia's history, from the time of the Occupation in 1890, this country has been developed and run by Rhodesians. After the Matabele Rebellion, Lord Summer, in the Judicial Committee of the Privy Council, decided on 29th July 1891 that, since conquest was by the Company's arms, and the Crown had made no contribution to the occupation, administration or conquest of Rhodesia, the Company's rights were established.

Since 1923, when self-government was granted, the Rhodesian Government has been responsible for the country's internal affairs and, to a large measure, her external relationships – particularly in the field of commerce. Her relations with Britain were conducted, not through the Colonial Office, but through the Dominions Office, and, later, the Commonwealth Relations Office, that Department of the British Government which acts as Britain's spokesman to independent countries of the Commonwealth. Unlike other territories in Africa to which Britain has granted Independence in recent years, Rhodesia, in view of her fully self-governing status, has never been administered by the British Colonial Service or, to use a common term, by 'expatriates'; the Civil Service, Police, Army and Air Force are locally based and regard the country they serve as their home. It goes without saying that the immigrants who have come to Rhodesia steadily throughout the years in search of a better future would not have done so unless they had good reason to trust in numerous assurances that their permanent place, in a Rhodesia under responsible government, was assured.

It is a fact that, if the ill-fated Federation of Southern Rhodesia, Northern Rhodesia and Nyasaland, as these countries were known at the time, had not been contrived by the British Government, Rhodesia would have attained her Independence in the early years of the 1950's. At that time, Rhodesia, acting in good faith, did not press her claim but agreed to co-operate with her northern neighbours, within a Federation, for the common good.

It was at about this time that Rhodesia began to experience the effects of what a British Prime Minister chose to call the 'wind of change'. It became obvious that there had occurred a striking *volte-face* in Britain's policy towards Africa in that she seemed bent, in an endeavour to placate the demands of certain states, on ridding herself of her responsibilities in Africa; on granting Independence, with hastily drafted constitutions, to the leaders of certain African countries who, through acts of terrorism and intimidation, had 'demonstrated' what Britain regarded as popular support. A host of newly 'independent' African states mushroomed into existence, not one of which could claim to have reached the standards of political or economic maturity attained by Rhodesia many years before.

Rhodesia watched with anxiety the effects of an early hand-over of responsibility to immature and ill-trained hands. One Government after another tottered; constitutions were torn up or modified to permit one-party dictatorships; the Congo fragmented into ghastly chaos; thousands of innocent people were murdered in Rwanda;

a Prime Minister slain in Burundi; a Government overthrown in a bloody coup in Zanzibar; violent disturb-
ances in the Central African Republic, in Togo, and in
the former British possessions in East Africa; the suc-
cession of military coups; the carnage in the Sudan –
and numerous other examples of breakdown. The flames
of disorder which were flaring through Africa, fanned
by Communist propaganda and unchecked by the new
rulers, licked even at Rhodesia's door, where they were
halted by a Government which is determined that the
peoples of Rhodesia will never be subjected to the in-
dignities and terror which have been suffered in African
states to the north.

When the Federation showed signs of breaking up,
through forces which Britain did nothing to control or
guide, the Rhodesian Government pursued discussions
aimed at Independence; and these culminated in the
significant advance represented in the 1961 Constitution.

After the Federation was eventually dismantled by
the British Government – without the concurrence of the
Rhodesian Government, but nevertheless with its co-
operation – the two least developed territories, Zambia
and Malawi, were granted Independence. Rhodesia,
with her outstanding record and her advanced adminis-
trative, economic and political structure, remained subject to a Government six thousand miles away! A Government, moreover, that had never governed Rhodesia, nor
contributed directly to her development.

The question of Rhodesia's complete independence
from Britain had been actively pursued since the
war, and discussions culminated in the constitutional
conference leading to the 1961 Constitution. The
British Government was party to the conference and

Constitution, and Rhodesians were led to believe that the 1961 Constitution would lead to full Independence.

This Constitution had been accepted not only by the Rhodesian and British Governments but also by the major African Nationalist parties, who saw in it a positive constitutional road which would lead them eventually to full satisfaction of their needs. But such a peaceful road was unacceptable to those other countries who saw in the Nationalists a means to an end – an end which meant the destruction of all that had been built up in Rhodesia over the years. External pressures were brought to bear, and the Nationalists, after having already accepted the Constitution, rejected it within a few days. The Constitution, in effect, provided for ever-increasing African participation in Parliament as more and more black Rhodesians achieved the necessary qualifications and acquired the responsibility for the vote by virtue of education, earning power and property ownership. It enshrined rule by the majority of those persons competent to exercise a vote. It was accepted by all the responsible peoples of Rhodesia as the Constitution on the basis of which Rhodesia would be granted her Independence.

But this was not to be; for as the negotiations proceeded throughout 1964 and into 1965 it became clear that the British Government, which itself had drafted the Constitution, was by this time no longer concerned with the merits of Rhodesia's case; it was to be guided only by expediency in an attempt to preserve the Commonwealth by capitulating to the demands of certain of its members.

Of Britain's attitude there can be no doubt; for whereas the previous British Government was prepared to rely on ambiguity to cloud the issues, before taking office as Britain's Prime Minister Mr Wilson had had no hesitation in defining his party's policy towards Rhodesia in a letter to Dr Mutasa in 1964. He wrote: 'The Labour Party is totally opposed to granting Independence to Southern Rhodesia so long as the Government of that country remains under the control of the white minority.'

Coupled with this, the British Premier's martially worded warning to the Rhodesian public, in an attempt to undermine their confidence in their elected Government, on the consequences of unilateral action by Rhodesia in the matter of Independence at a time when the negotiations between the two Governments were still in progress did little to restore confidence in Rhodesians that Britain was working honestly and objectively towards a solution of the problem.

The choice the British Government attempted to portray was a simple one between the indefinite continuation of 'white rule' or the 'democracy' of one man, one vote. This was by no means the real choice. The choice was between the continuation of responsible government, the orderly and increasing participation of black Rhodesians in a Government which is working towards the advancement of all Rhodesians regardless of colour, or a premature hand-over to majority rule, which in effect meant extreme black Nationalist rule on the principle of one man, one vote.

In this regard, it can be said that the following statements by the Chiefs, who are the traditional leaders of Rhodesia's African peoples, made to the British Government early in 1964, echo the views of the majority of black Rhodesians:

'We, as chiefs and leaders of the people, have one, and only one, desire, and that is to live in peace and harmony without this chaos and murder that seems to be the order of the day. As far as the granting of Independence to Southern Rhodesia is concerned, we abhor one man, one vote and absolutely recoil at the thought of this because of the chaos and murder that is bound to result.'

And:

'We would press for immediate Independence for Southern Rhodesia in terms of the existing Constitution, which allows for devolvement and progress. We have seen the events that have already taken place in other countries . . .'

By now the seeming futility of the prolonged negotiations and the dawning realization that the British Government was conceding more and more to the demands of countries hostile towards Rhodesia were having their effect on Rhodesia. Foreign investment to assist towards the further development of the country's vast natural resources was slowing considerably as would-be investors hesitated, fearful lest Rhodesia was forced by Britain to surrender the reins of responsible government. African Nationalists, spurred on by Communist influences, stepped up their acts of vandalism and intimidation, confident that while they were so doing Britain would afford them protection. This increased the determination of responsible Rhodesians, black and white, mindful of the effects of Britain's policies elsewhere in Africa, to do everything possible to maintain their standards of civilization.

In the British autumn of 1965 negotiations reached a critical stage and, while there could be little room left for doubt as to the lack of sincerity of the British Government's approach to the issue, the Rhodesian Prime Minister proceeded to London to meet the British Premier in October 1965, in a last effort to resolve the deadlock.

It was on this occasion that any lingering doubts were set aside, for it transpired that Rhodesia's leaders had not been invited to London for negotiations in the accepted sense of that word but to be told of conditions which, it must be assumed, the British Premier expected would prove unacceptable to the Government of Rhodesia.

In essence, the British condition for the granting of Independence was that Rhodesia would have to accept the following five principles:

1. Unimpeded progress to majority rule.
2. The provision of guarantees that there would not be any retrogressive amendments to the Constitution to retard African advancement.
3. An immediate increase in the political representation of Africans.
4. The end of racial discrimination.
5. Evidence to the satisfaction of the British Government that any basis of Independence was acceptable to the people of Rhodesia as a whole.

If Mr Wilson considered that this ultimatum would have forced the Rhodesian Ministers to abandon the discussions, he was guilty of an error of judgement. It was pointed out by the Rhodesian Premier that his Government did not oppose the first condition. In fact he offered to guarantee this under a solemn international treaty. Rhodesia's only concern in this regard was to

ensure a measured rate of progress best suited to protect
the interests of all the peoples of Rhodesia. The second
condition was met by the Rhodesian Government, far
from demonstrating any desire to retard advance, offering a Senate composed of African Chiefs. Rhodesians
had already accepted it, and in any event any such
amendments required a two-thirds majority under the
1961 Constitution.

In answer to the third condition, and additionally
to this proposed Senate, the Rhodesian Government
offered a virtual enfranchisement on the lower roll of
the entire population.

It was agreed that as far as the fourth condition was
concerned there should be continued progress towards
ending racial discrimination, and the Rhodesian Government indicated that this was a continuing process of
change. Their policies would continue to be progressive
in this regard.

On the fifth condition it is worth recalling that
Rhodesia had already consulted her African peoples
through their Chiefs, who, in speaking for the majority
of black Rhodesians, had been in favour of Independence on the basis of the 1961 Constitution.

But it transpired that the British Government could
not find a basis for negotiation even after this demonstration of Rhodesia's willingness to meet Mr Wilson
at least half-way; the talks broke down.

To the Press, Rhodesia's Prime Minister had these
comments to make before his return to Rhodesia:

'Every time we moved towards them they moved
further away from us. The British Government has
categorically stated that it no longer believes that
the 1961 Constitution is an appropriate basis for

Independence. This is contrary to everything we have been led to believe in the past.'

But the curtain had not yet fallen. Conscious of the warmth of feeling exhibited by much of the British public for the Rhodesian Premier, Mr Smith, whose sincerity and honesty had impressed the British voter deeply, Mr Wilson, in an eleventh-hour endeavour to display to the world at large that he was doing 'everything humanly possible' to avert a crisis (which was largely of his own making), announced his intention to fly to the Rhodesian capital for further discussion.

Once again the Rhodesian Government willingly entered into negotiations with the British Premier, as a result of which it was announced in Salisbury that both Governments had agreed to establish a Royal Commission whose function it would be to determine if an acceptable Constitution could be achieved. The Rhodesians welcomed what appeared to be a change of heart on the British side, and, confident in the righteousness of their case, hopefully looked towards the establishment of such a Commission as the final leg of the long road to Independence. But they were sorely disappointed, for when the British Premier returned to London he made it clear that even should the Royal Commission submit a unanimous report in favour of Rhodesia's claim to Independence the British Government would not be obliged to accept it.

It was now quite plain for all to see that the earlier doubts and mistrust of Britain's intentions towards Rhodesia were completely justified. Their exposure suggested that Rhodesia was merely being used by Britain as an expendable pawn in the gambit to maintain the goodwill of less mature Commonwealth countries.

It became finally and absolutely clear that if Rhodesia
was to take her rightful place on the road to further
prosperity and maintain the standards she had set herself by her own endeavours during forty-two years of
self-government she would have to leave the path laid
down for her by Britain. Rhodesia could not by her
inaction allow indecision and doubt to continue until
she was demolished, as was the Federation of Rhodesia
and Nyasaland. This was the spectre that hung before
her, and thus it was that Independence was declared
on 11th November 1965.

Much of the furore following the assumption of Independence is based on the question of 'legality', and of
basic human rights for Africans as well as Europeans.

The Constitution of 1965 retains the provisions of the
1961 Constitution regarding the Declaration of Rights
and the Constitutional Council. The latter scrutinizes
legislation to ensure that it is not discriminatory. The
Declaration of Rights contains detailed and extensive
documentation of the fundamental rights and freedoms
of all individuals, of whatever race, tribe, place of
origin, political opinion, colour or creed, to life, liberty,
security of the person, enjoyment of property and protection of the law; freedom of conscience, of expression,
of assembly and association, and respect for private
and family life.

Contrary to the world's belief, Africans, Asians,
Coloureds and Europeans in Rhodesia have equal rights
to the franchise and to seats in Parliament. The vote
and all sixty-five seats in Parliament are open, solely
on the basis of merit and ability, regardless of race. No
basic human rights are specially reserved by law to any
section of the population. Opportunity is likewise open

to all individuals to advance in other spheres, according
to merit and ability. Africans in Rhodesia probably
enjoy a greater measure of practical freedom and opportunity than in any African state.

The Rhodesian Government's record in the advancement of Africans is not excelled anywhere to the north.
It has to be recognized that the burden of this has been
carried almost entirely by the small white section of
the population, who, through their enterprise, capital,
skills and ability, have raised this modern state up from
a primitive wilderness. This development has occurred
during a single lifetime.

The laws of Rhodesia have been conceived, enacted
and enforced by Rhodesia, in her own right. The country
has been financed and developed by Rhodesians and not
by Britain. During over forty years of efficient self-
government Britain has not legislated for this country
save at Rhodesia's request except on two occasions and
in both of these Britain quickly contacted the Rhodesian
Government for its agreement to the action taken.

In this context of Rhodesia's record, where was the
morality or legality of Britain's claim to stand in the
way of Rhodesia's further progress and her full Independence? Where is the morality today in Britain's
campaign to destroy what has been built up by Rhodesians through their own efforts and resources? Where
is the justice in Britain's claiming the right to plunder
what has been built up by one section of the population and transfer it to the hands of another section
which – despite equal rights and opportunities – has not
shown itself capable of sustaining it? Where is the
morality or legality in the misappropriation or the theft
of Rhodesia's hard-earned foreign assets, and thereafter

charging Rhodesia with defaulting in her international obligations?

The referendum held in November 1964, on the question of Independence on the basis of the 1961 Constitution returned a majority of 89.1 per cent in favour – a record unequalled in Rhodesian electoral history. This majority was greater than that which voted for the 1961 Constitution itself.

The Independence which is Rhodesia's right required the technical assent of Her Majesty the Queen. Britain has done nothing for Rhodesia which could justify any right to determine Rhodesia's destiny. The circumstances by which she acquired this technical right were entirely fortuitous, and followed from the natural attachment Rhodesians felt for Britain and the Monarchy. The Government which assumed Independence was legally elected, with a sweeping victory.

The Constitution of 1961 was designed to eliminate the British Government's control over Rhodesian affairs except for certain matters relating to international financial commitments and treaty obligations. The White Paper on the Southern Rhodesia Constitution, Part I, issued by Her Majesty's Stationery Office, London, states explicitly on page 3 that the 1961 Constitution 'will eliminate all the reserved powers at present vested in the Government of the United Kingdom, save for certain matters set out in paragraph 50'. This paragraph 50 in the White Paper became section 32 of the Southern Rhodesia (Constitution) Order in Council, 1961, which covers only the following restrictive powers:

(a) to alter to the injury of stockholders any of the undertakings given by the Government of Southern

Rhodesia Government stock registered under the Colonial Stock Act, 1877 or any Act amending or replacing the same; or

(b) to involve a departure from any obligation imposed on Her Majesty in relation to Southern Rhodesia by any treaty, convention, agreement or arrangement relating to any country or international or similar organization.

It is clear, therefore, that, by virtue of the 1961 Constitution, Rhodesia was independent, save only in regard to matters concerning the Colonial Stock Act and international treaty obligations.

Section 20 (2) conferred on the Rhodesian legislature power to make 'laws having extra-territorial operation', within the framework of the Federation. This surely foreshadowed Rhodesia's moral right to Independence, and, incidentally, to appoint her own diplomatic representatives.

The Legislature of Rhodesia, in terms of section 6, was to 'consist of Her Majesty and a Legislative Assembly'. The British Government ceased to figure in the 1961 Constitution after the granting thereof.

One further vital power was embodied in section 42, which gave Rhodesia complete executive powers over all her affairs except over matters dealt with in section 32 (above). Section 42 reads:

'The executive authority of Southern Rhodesia is vested in Her Majesty and may be exercised on Her Majesty's behalf by the Governor or such persons as may be authorized in that behalf by the Governor, or any law of the Legislature.'

The last phrase is the key to Rhodesia's Independence, which, under the 1961 Constitution, was within the competence and powers of Her Majesty and without the British Government entering the picture.

It is clear, therefore, that the contention of 'illegality' in regard to Rhodesia's action is technical rather than substantive. Rhodesia assumed her Independence because this was her sovereign right, built upon her unexcelled record of self-government. Rhodesia is a mature country with a long history of freedom.

It is noteworthy that section 26 (2) of the 1923 Constitution of Rhodesia gave her the power to repeal certain Orders-in-Council of the British Government having effect over Rhodesia except for certain specified matters.

This section 26 (2) reads as follows:

'A Law passed by the Legislature may repeal or alter any of the provisions of these Our Letters Patent, save those contained in this section, and those contained in section 28 (relating to the reservation of Bills), section 39–47 (relating to Native Administration), and section 55 (relating to the salary of the Governor), and may likewise repeal or alter any of the provisions of any Order in Our Privy Council extending to Southern Rhodesia other than provisions affecting any matter mentioned in this subsection:

'Provided, however, that no proposed Law for the constitution of a Legislative Council in pursuance of section 2 of these Our Letters Patent shall repeal or alter any of the provisions relating to the Legislative Council contained in these Our Letters Patent, and such provisions shall not be repealed or altered save by a Law passed by both Houses of the Legislature, after the constitution of a Legislative Council as aforesaid:

'Provided further that no proposed Law for the repeal or alteration of any such provisions of these Our Letters

Patent as may be repealed or altered by the Legislature as aforesaid shall be valid unless it shall be affirmed by not less than two-thirds of the total number of Members of each House of the Legislature, or, pending the constitution of a Legislative Council, of the Legislative Assembly.'

The assurances given at the time of the 1961 Constitutional negotiations that Rhodesia would have her Independence on the basis of this Constitution are confirmed in the quotation from the White Paper, given previously, to the effect that it was designed to eliminate all the reserved powers save only for those relating to the Colonial Stock Act. The British Government repudiated its promise and demanded concessions which would have the result of destroying Rhodesia as we know it. Rhodesia was, therefore, left with no option but to cut the tie unilaterally.

This event, on 11th November 1965, marked the turning-point in the brush-fires of unrestrained nationalism that is sweeping down Africa with its engulfing tragedy of Communist subversion. Rhodesia has turned the flames back – and incurred the wrath of the Afro-Asians and those who dance to their tune – but the world will some day realize that the lower does not govern the higher; incompetence should not subordinate competence; licence ought not to supplant realistic freedom; poverty and sloth should not dictate to capital and enterprise; nor ignorance to skill and experience.

There are few countries in Africa today that can claim to equal Rhodesia's record of democracy and racial harmony. There are even fewer who would attempt to substantiate a claim to match Rhodesia's history of tranquillity and steady economic progress since self-government was granted in 1923. In the space of only forty-two years Rhodesia's economic progress, political advancement and judicial integrity can be measured by a yardstick which not only surpasses every country in Africa north of the Zambezi, but that of many countries elsewhere in the world.

The so-called 'illegality' which other countries would hold against Rhodesia is shown to be a myth. The assumption of Independence merely confirmed the factual position.

According to a South African Q.C., Mr D. Molteno, 'any constitution rested essentially on general acquiescence. A constitution was not law because somebody had made it, but because it had been accepted'. There is no doubt whatever that the Rhodesian populace as a whole has accepted the 1965 Constitution. In general, peace and good order have continued to reign throughout—an example unexcelled in Africa. Both international law and the United Nations Charter provide for the recognition of a *de facto* Government once it has been accepted by the people. By virtue of the peace and calm that has prevailed in the country, it is Rhodesia's demonstrated and undoubted right to be recognized forthwith.

The historian Lord Acton, commenting on the American Declaration of Independence, wrote: 'It was from America that the plain ideas that men ought to mind their own business, and that the nation is responsible to Heaven for the acts of the State . . . burst forth like a conqueror upon the world they were destined to transform, under the title of the Rights of Man . . . and the principle gained ground, that a nation can never abandon its fate to an authority it cannot control.' Rhodesia has no intention of doing so.

3

Negotiating with Wilson – and Bottomley

Having been forced, therefore, to take the decision we did on the 11th November, it may be of interest to reflect on the progress of negotiations which brought about the final communiqué from No. 10 Downing Street, which read as follows:

'The Prime Minister and the Commonwealth Secretary have held during this week a series of discussions with the Prime Minister and other Ministers of Rhodesia, during which they have examined frankly and thoroughly all aspects of the questions of Rhodesia's independence. The British Ministers have described the constitutional principles which the British Government would regard as the essential basis on which they could recommend to Parliament the grant of sovereign independence to Rhodesia; and the Rhodesian Ministers have indicated the reasons for which they feel unable to accept these principles in the measure required by the British Government. Despite intensive discussion, no means have been found of reconciling the opposing views. No further meeting has been arranged.'

As we have seen, the principles mentioned in the communiqué consisted of:

(i) The principles and intention of unimpeded progress to majority rule, already enshrined in the 1961 Constitution, would have to be maintained and guaranteed.

(ii) There would also have to be guarantees against retrogressive amendment of the Constitution.

(iii) There would have to be immediate improvement in the political status of the African population.

(iv) There would have to be progress towards ending racial discrimination.

(v) The British Government would need to be satisfied that any basis proposed for Independence was acceptable to the people of Rhodesia as a whole.

The last principle had been discussed between the Conservative Government and Mr Ian Smith, and Mr Smith had told them that he intended consulting the Chiefs and Headmen, who represented the population living in the Tribal Trust areas numbering in excess of three million. Discussions did take place between Conservative Ministers and Mr Smith, as to whether Chiefs and Headmen would be the only ones consulted; the Conservative Ministers suggested that Kraal Heads should also be taken into consideration in arriving at a decision by the tribesmen. Mr Smith made it perfectly clear to Sir Alec Douglas-Home that, if the suggestion of bringing Kraal Heads into the discussions was contrary to the custom and was not acceptable to the Chiefs, he would not go to such lengths.

As is known, the Dombashawa Indaba took place, at which the decision of the Chiefs was to the effect that they agreed to Independence on the 1961 Constitution and were in support of Mr Ian Smith and his Government.

Mr Bottomley has stated that he spoke to certain Chiefs while he was here and they intimated they did not agree with the decision. This again illustrates, so clearly, that the customs and ways of the African people are not known to the British Government. According to African custom, any decision made is a communal one; immediately the community has decided on an issue, then in terms of true democracy the minority accept the majority view, which is put forward as the community's unanimous view.

The Indaba lasted for several days and the Chiefs discussed the matter entirely on their own. When they arrived at the decision it was sent to the British Government. This decision was not accepted by either the Conservative leaders or the Labour leaders.

As no conclusions had been reached after the visits of Lord Gardiner and Mr Bottomley, and later Mr Cledwyn Hughes, to this country, Mr Ian Smith considered that it was necessary for him to proceed to London, in order to have final talks with a view to getting our Independence and an agreement with Britain. As he indicated to Mr Wilson that he wished for a final decision to be arrived at, and he was not prepared to agree to the policy of procrastination being pursued by the British Government, I was asked to accompany the Prime Minister to London, and, knowing the background of what had transpired, we entered into discussions with Mr Bottomley and his advisers at the Commonwealth Relations Office.

It must be remembered that, historically, Rhodesia could have had her Independence on various occasions. It was offered to her during the war but was refused pending the settlement of the conflagration.

When I was a back-bencher in Parliament between 1948 and 1953, various discussions took place concerning the Independence of Rhodesia and a Select Committee was set up, under the chairmanship of Sir Ray Stockil, when evidence was taken from all sections of the public to decide on the Constitution Rhodesia would have on her independence. During this period, however, the ill-fated idea of a Federation was bandied about; and by virtue of the fact that it was the intention of the three countries to get together, Rhodesia again did not press for the Independence to which she was entitled, and agreed to participate in the Federal experiment.

During the period of Federation, thoughts of our Independence again became very pertinent and negotiations started for a new Constitution which terminated in the 1961 Constitution. As to whether this was to be an independence Constitution has been argued for some considerable time, but I am perfectly satisfied, from the statements made during the referendum in Rhodesia, that the public were advised by the then Rhodesian Government that this Constitution would be the Constitution which would last for 300 years, and would be the Constitution that would give Rhodesia Independence. These statements were never denied by the British Government.

Examining in retrospect what happened during that period and afterwards, I am fully convinced that in dealing with British Government it is essential to commit any agreement in writing and never to accept a spoken word as binding.

After the Rhodesian Front was returned to power in this country in 1962, on the mandate to obtain our

Independence, negotiations commenced. Discussions took place between Mr Winston Field and the British Government, and later with Mr Ian Smith and the British Government. The progress of these negotiations are public knowledge, as they have been published in the form of a White Paper; therefore I do not intend to go over any of these facts.

It became obvious, after Lord Gardiner and Mr Bottomley had travelled to Rhodesia followed by Mr Cledwyn Hughes' visit, that the whole attitude of the British Government was one of deliberate procrastination, there was no intention to get to any finality. Owing to this continued frustration, it was obvious that some action had to be taken, which was why Mr Smith stated that he was going to London to get some final decision from the British Government.

It soon became clear to me that there was considerable prejudice against us emanating from the officials who were advising the British Government and evidenced by the utterances made by Mr Bottomley. It became obvious that the British attitude was unbalanced by reason of the fact that the Rhodesian Front held all fifty A Roll seats in the Rhodesia Parliament. They could not or would not appreciate that it would be highly unlikely for such a situation to occur again. Negotiations, therefore, were always clouded with this fact and I honestly feel that had the Rhodesian Front won only forty seats out of sixty-five the question of the blocking third, which became so prominent in British thinking, would in all probability not have arisen. The British delegates could not, or would not, appreciate that the discussions were in respect of a Constitution that we hoped would carry Rhodesia through for a considerable period of its history; the whole of their attitude was centred on the present position and their arguments were based on these facts.

It also became perfectly plain that we were up against tremendous difficulties simply because our faces were white. *At one meeting when Mr Bottomley was in the chair I accused him of this fact and pointed out that had our faces been black the points which had been set out as the five principles would never have been contemplated and that our Independence would have been given without any argument at all.* This appeared to touch a guilty conscience, as this was the only time that there was any acrimony in the talks with us, for Mr Bottomley became extremely irate at my suggestion, proving to me that what I had said to him was the truth and he did not like it expressed in so many words. It was also obvious that at the meetings we had in which Mr Bottomley was in the chair we were making no progress whatsoever. Mr Bottomley had no mandate, as I could see, to make any concession, and in fact he retreated in some instances—so much so that he led us to believe that the 1961 Constitution could never really be a basis for our Independence!

Mr Smith, on the other hand, was always prepared to concede where he thought it would be for the benefit of Rhodesia, and showed that we were genuinely endeavouring to reach an amicable solution which would culminate in our getting Independence with the agreement of the British Government.

Certain concessions that were made could have led to considerable criticism on returning to Rhodesia, as they were, in all probability, further than the Rhodesian public were prepared to go. For instance, it was suggested that we extended the franchise on the B Roll to enable all duly qualified taxpayers to have a vote. Be that as it may, these actions all go to show the genuineness of Mr Smith and the irreconcilable attitude adopted by the British Government.

Two days of talks ensued which brought forth absolutely nothing. It was therefore obvious that if any breakthrough was to occur it could only happen with Mr Wilson present. Thus it was decided that we would continue discussions with Mr Wilson. Mr Ian Smith stated that he thought that it was not necessary for officials to be present and that any decisions arrived at would be made by the Ministers. This was agreed upon by Mr Wilson, and the meetings we had with him were not interrupted by note-passing and whispering officials.

The atmosphere was entirely different in the talks we had with Mr Wilson, because it was obvious that we were talking to a person who knew his brief and was prepared to discuss the matter in an endeavour to arrive at a solution, if possible. *During these talks the only real contributions came from Mr Wilson on the British side, neither Lord Gardiner nor Mr Bottomley making any contribution whatsoever.*

The five principles were again referred to. The first principle, as far as the Rhodesian members were concerned, was inherent in the 1961 Constitution, and therefore we had complied and were complying with it.

It was clear to all thinking people that the Royal Commission was another ruse to delay a decision and was merely being established to enable the British Government to call another Constitutional Conference, or to commence another round of protracted negotiations. Further, Mr Wilson made it perfectly clear that even if the Commission reported that the people of Rhodesia unanimously accepted the 1961 Constitution, as far as the British Government was concerned it would only be considered as a bargaining counter.

Much play has been made by Mr Wilson on the final telephone call between himself and Mr Smith—which, incidentally, was tape-recorded and divulged to the world at large without the consent of Mr Smith. Even with this conversation, a study of it will show that at no time was it fundamentally agreed that the British Government would give Independence on the 1961 Constitution, if the Commission reported unanimously that the people of Rhodesia as a whole accepted it.

Bearing in mind all the points which I have mentioned leading up to our decision, I think any reasonable person will realize that the Rhodesian Government, through the deliberate obstructionist attitude of the British Government, had no option but to make the decision it did and to assume its democratic rights on the 11th November.

It must be appreciated that this decision was not taken lightly. Hours of discussion and argument took place prior to it. Having been at the Conference in London and having heard both Mr Wilson and Mr Smith agree that the attitudes of the Governments were irreconcilable, action was necessary, and necessary quickly, in order to save Rhodesia. It had been appreciated that sanctions would be applied and that the average Rhodesian would have to suffer, but in order to save this part of the world from the ultimate chaos of Communism it was necessary to stop the sense of frustration which had been created in the minds of all Rhodesians and the vacillation which appeared to be the dedicated policy of the British Government.

Mr Wilson conceded that, although the Rhodesian members were not prepared to agree to the repeal of the Land Apportionment Act, our disagreement on this point was not as great as on the others. He indicated that there was no early prospect of majority rule and that there was no intention, on the Rhodesian part, to accelerate the education of Africans for this purpose. This was the point that amazed me, as Mr Wilson had asked us whether we would accelerate the educational programme for the purpose of enabling Africans to get on the Voters' Roll and, as it appeared to me, for no other purpose. Mr Smith quite rightly indicated that in Rhodesia education was not given for that purpose, but was given for the benefit of the individual concerned, so that he could take his place in the economic life of the country. It appeared to me to be extremely peculiar that anyone could be so narrow in his outlook as to think solely of the political position and not the economic position and well-being of the country.

I quote from the official release of the second meeting with Mr Wilson:

'Rhodesia might be pressing on with education for Africans, generally, but this was not for political reasons but in recognition of the intrinsic desirability of education. The United Kingdom Government could not countenance a transfer of sovereignty on the basis of so slender a guarantee of early majority rule.'

Concerning principle 3, that there would have to be an immediate improvement in the political status of the African population, the British Government could not accept that the creation of a Senate would fulfil this requirement. They insisted upon the Lower House having twelve extra Africans so as to bring in a blocking third—this blocking third not only to be in respect of the entrenched clauses of the Constitution, but in respect of all amendments to the Constitution, special further safeguards to be inserted in the Constitution in respect of the entrenched clauses. The suggestion of the expansion of the B Roll was not decisive enough, as it did not provide any more seats for the Africans.

As far as the fifth principle was concerned, Mr Smith quite rightly indicated that, until the other four were agreed to, it was not much use putting forward suggestions as to how the British Government would be satisfied if the Rhodesian people as a whole accepted the Constitution. This point, however, became a focal one in subsequent meetings in Rhodesia.

Mr Wilson was determined to bring about a Constitutional Conference, which he had virtually promised to the Commonwealth at a previous Prime Ministers' Conference.

Whilst in Rhodesia he intimated that if the Royal Commission found that the people of Rhodesia as a whole were in favour of Independence under the 1961 Constitution, Independence on that basis would be granted. On his return to London, however, after visiting Zambia and Tanzania and other African Commonwealth countries, and presumably consulting his Cabinet, his attitude changed and he indicated that the findings of the Commission could not be regarded as binding upon the British Government and, further, he reserved his right to call a Constitutional Conference if the Commission indicated that the people as a whole did not agree.

This was in spite of the fact that a week earlier he had stated in Salisbury that a Constitutional Conference was a waste of time.

When it became obvious that the decisions of the two Governments were irreconcilable, Mr Wilson indicated to us what would happen if we were to assume our Independence unilaterally. The whole theme of his dissertation was that Britain would have to do something, otherwise the United Nations and the Commonwealth would take it out of British hands. He painted a gory picture of race riots right through Africa, with the British fighting kith and kin because of our action, and generally did everything he could to scare us. Listening to his harangue, it became obvious that the whole of the British attitude showed their fear of what the United Nations would do and the fear of what might happen not only in Rhodesia but in the whole of Africa, in the event of the threatened action being taken.

There was no suggestion, at that stage, that Britain was going to be the instigator of sanctions and bring about diplomatic pressure and threats of dire consequences if the rest of the world did not support her. The whole attitude was that Britain would be forced to take action to prevent the United Nations from doing anything.

Everybody knows what really happened and how Britain went crying to the United Nations immediately, asking for their total help. Everyone also knows what Britain has done since, how pressures have been brought upon other Governments and upon people.

The actions of Britain are far in excess of anything that Mr Wilson suggested to us at the penultimate meeting we had with him. To indicate the attitude he put across to the meeting, I quote from the official record:

'Mr Lardner-Burke said that surely the consequences which the Prime Minister had described would stem from the action taken by the United Kingdom; it would be the United Kingdom whose lead would be followed. If the United Kingdom did not take action of the kind in question, the adverse reactions would be unlikely.'

Mr Wilson said he did not agree; but I think it is obvious to anybody that had Britain adopted the attitude which I suggested, the vindictiveness and punitive measures which have been showered upon us would never have taken place.

It was clear now that the end had come. Not even the biggest optimist could see any future in Rhodesia if the position remained as it was. It was certain that Britain intended to hand Rhodesia over to the black Rhodesians, without any consideration for what would happen to those people who had made Rhodesia what it was.

It was obvious that as far as the British Government was concerned, the Europeans were expendable and we knew that we had to act quickly.

4

Ian Smith in Britain

It was incredible to me the way in which the British people took the Rhodesian Prime Minister, Ian Smith, to their hearts. During the period that we were in Britain we travelled from Rhodesia House to No. 10 Downing Street or the Commonwealth Relations Office daily and we usually found a crowd waiting in the Strand or at Downing Street whenever the Prime Minister arrived. The reception was extremely warm and the absence of the usual right-wing extremists was commented upon continuously. Only on one occasion during the whole of the period we were in Britain did any active demonstration take place. That was outside 10 Downing Street at a time when we were attending a meeting.

Mr Wilson's reaction to all this was remarkable. On the Thursday evening a reception was given to Mr Smith in Rhodesia House and a considerable number of prominent people, including the Secretary of State for Commonwealth Relations and Members of Parliament, attended. Everyone was very friendly. Mr Smith left at approximately eight o'clock to appear on I.T.V. Some forty of us remained at Rhodesia House to watch the television interview. We were extremely impressed with it; more particularly as one of our most voluble critics, Mr. Colin

Legum, appeared to have by far the worst of it and was seen to be mopping his brow in the end. Presumably he was utterly exasperated because he had been unable to flurry the Prime Minister at all, and the answers he got were honest, truthful, and not what he had expected. It was a masterly performance. Before we could go down the stairs on our way home, the telephone began to ring and it continued to do so until approximately 1.30 in the morning, with people sending in congratulations and support for Mr Smith and his stand on Rhodesia.

The next morning the telegrams and letters started to arrive, and they appeared in their hundreds. Some were particularly interesting and a number expressed the wish that Mr Smith should be Britain's Prime Minister! Many people told of their exasperation at the attitude of Mr Wilson. They appreciated to the full the case put forward by Mr Smith, and were supporting his approach to the Rhodesian question.

All this had an effect on Mr Wilson, because, the next time we met, Mr Wilson congratulated Mr Smith on his performance and wanted to know whether he had had much television practice in Rhodesia. It was obvious that he was very impressed by the broadcast and was worried that another appearance of that nature would rally more of the British public to Mr Smith's side. It was only natural therefore that many people should think that the refusal of the B.B.C. to allow Mr Smith to appear on television at a later date must have been, directly or indirectly, at the request of Mr Wilson.

In London one can expect crowds to gather at the slightest pretext and there was usually one when Mr Smith left Rhodesia House or arrived at one of the Government offices. The most impressive incidents

c

occurred, however, when driving to Downing Street.
Whenever the motor-car stopped at the traffic lights, or
slowed down for a crowd of people, we would see men
taking off their hats and giving the thumbs-up sign or the
victory sign, and numerous shouts of good luck were
heard. Wherever we went there was always a sign of
encouragement, with people wishing us good luck and
hoping that Rhodesia would be able to solve the problems she was up against. I honestly think that these
demonstrations worried Mr Wilson considerably, and
there is no doubt that he was fed with reports indicating
the popularity of Mr Smith in London.

Whilst over there, Mr Smith was always in the company of a security officer, and I became friendly with
a few of them and discussed matters on various occasions. They told me that they had done this type of
work with various Ministers who had come over to
Britain, but they had never seen such spontaneous support and encouragement as the public had given Mr
Smith during the period that he was in London. In the
bars, where Mr Smith's visit was the topic of the day,
the manner in which he had been taken into the hearts
of the Londoners and the rest of the British people was
made manifestly plain. It was most encouraging, and I
am satisfied that this visit to London made a very
marked impression upon the people of Britain, and it
is because of this that we have the support of the
British public to the extent that we have today.

I remember on the day we were leaving there was
a large crowd outside Rhodesia House; in the Strand
they were standing ten deep and, generally, it was
difficult to move. Out of Rhodesia House came Mr
Smith, to a considerable amount of cheering, and got

into the car. I followed him and, just prior to leaving, a woman put her head into the window and said: 'Mr Smith, go back and save your country and then come back and save ours.' This was greeted with great acclamation and appeared to be the attitude of the people standing there at the time.

Since returning to Rhodesia, letters, telegrams and other messages of goodwill have poured in from all over the world. There is no doubt that the reason for this terrific response by the man in the street is because of his feeling for fair play and the knowledge that Rhodesia has not had a fair deal from Britain. It is now dawning on everyone that the attitude of Britain is one of a bully endeavouring to overpower some small individual with its overwhelming strength. The spirit of the British people is now becoming manifest, as it did when Britain was previously in trouble. The manner in which Independence has been given to various other African territories and the way in which these territories have treated Britain has made the average Briton lose his self-confidence. The fact that we have taken a stand, in spite of the dire threats that have been made against us, has been welcomed by many of the British. Rhodesia is determined that she will not be undermined by the socialistic policy of the British Government; we are determined to prevent alignment with Communism in the southern part of Africa. We are not prepared to be forced to hand over this beautiful country to people who have no ability to govern. The British Government requires the hand-over of Rhodesia in order to appease the Afro-Asian group and our refusal to be blackmailed stands in sharp contrast to their policy for twenty years.

Since the 11th November the British Government

has shown unexampled pettiness. We were warned that Britain would be forced to take certain steps if we declared our Independence, because if she did not the United Nations would take over. We then found that instructions were sent out by the British Government to all civil servants in Britain that under no circumstances should they fraternize with Rhodesians. Instructions were sent to all diplomats wherever Rhodesia was represented that they should ignore Rhodesian representatives. Not only were these instructions sent to the British diplomatic service but they were passed on to Commonwealth and other consular representatives.

Many examples of this pettiness have occurred since U.D.I., and it does seem that the British Government has done all in her power to interfere with everything that the Rhodesian Government wishes to do for the benefit of Rhodesia. This has meant that even in cases of an entirely non-political nature, efforts to make economic advances of benefit to all races in Rhodesia have been impeded because of Mr Wilson's political position. Attempts have been made to make it more difficult for Rhodesia to carry out schemes which are urgently needed for the economic improvement of the country even though these schemes are in no way controversial but dictated entirely by economic necessity.

As a rule, it is said that time is a great healer; but in this operation, as far as the British Government is concerned, it appears to be the opposite. The longer we carry on as we are, the more vindictive they become. Looking at the overall position, I don't think there is any doubt that this growing vindictiveness stems from the fact that certain prominent civil servants in the Foreign Office and the C.R.O. are now being criticized because of the inaccuracy of their advice to Ministers prior to the 11th November. It is obvious that the advice they gave was very unsatisfactory and their intelligence work extremely poor.

They seem to have suggested that the Rhodesian public was disunited and the majority of them were willing to get rid of Mr Ian Smith's Government. This meant that all that was required was a little pressure and the whole of the structure would collapse. They seem to have ignored the fact that the huge majority given to Mr Smith in the referendum held in 1963 indicated that the people were behind him. It was even more striking that the elections in 1965 gave his party every seat on the A Roll. It is impossible to understand how they could have arrived at the conclusion that there were more people prepared to overthrow the Rhodesian Government than there were prepared to back it. How wrong they were events have proved.

I know that when the Chief Justice visited Britain after the 11th November he advised Mr Wilson and Mr Bottomley, and presumably the senior officials, that they were completely wrong in their assessment of the Rhodesian people, but they did not accept this advice. The Conservatives, on the other hand, appear to have listened to the Chief Justice when he advised them in the same way, and they have taken an entirely different attitude since speaking to him and since certain of their members have visited Rhodesia. They appreciated the determination that had grown in the minds of the Rhodesian people, whose resolution had hardened since Mr Wilson had made his attitude plain. They knew that short of successful invasion, there was nothing that could break the spirit of Rhodesia. Therefore discussions were obviously necessary, particularly as the British economy has been hit harder than the Rhodesian economy.

The Labour Party did not deem it wise to send out any of its Members of Parliament except three who turned up with preconceived ideas bent on causing trouble and refusing to abide by the law of the land.

Mr Wilson again got his facts wrong over this affair. He made a statement on arrival in London from his meeting in Zambia with President Kaunda and alleged that certain grossly exaggerated incidents had taken place and queried why the police had allowed such a position to eventuate, indicating that the Government had been wrong in allowing the meeting if it had been illegal. The three Members of Parliament, on the other hand, praised the actions of the police and thanked them for what they had done.

Another interesting position arose when Mr Selwyn Lloyd was in Rhodesia. Questions were asked in the British Parliament about his visit, and Mr Wilson replied to the effect that he sincerely hoped that Mr Selwyn Lloyd would not call upon Mr Ian Smith as the Prime Minister of Rhodesia and in no way would acknowledge any Minister as a Minister of Rhodesia. In the same breath he said that he hoped Mr Selwyn Lloyd would put to the Rhodesian Prime Minister the British attitude to the censorship of the Press. In the one breath he indicated that there could be no recognition of the Rhodesian Government, and in the other he asked Mr Selwyn Lloyd to recognize the Rhodesian Government by speaking to the Prime Minister and other Ministers concerning regulations which they had made.

Throughout this affair we have suffered from the continued inaccuracy, pettiness, and straight slander of the

British Government. Our real need is to be understood and our case heard without rancour or prejudice. Mr Smith came to London to see that this was done. When he had put it to the Government he set out to explain his position to the Conservative Party.

5

Negotiations with Mr Heath and the Climax

The Leader of the Conservative Party, Mr Heath, wanted consultations with Mr Smith, as his party appeared to be worried about the outcome of the talks and the likelihood of complete breakdown. Mr Heath, therefore, asked Mr Smith if he would see him at his hotel suite on the Sunday, and I was invited to be present. The whole position was canvassed and it was obvious that Sir Alec Douglas-Home was fully aware of all the difficulties. It appeared, however, that the Conservatives had a new approach in the form of a treaty, so we discussed what they meant by a treaty. They apparently had in mind that we should enter into a solemn treaty to the effect that we would not pass any laws which would be retrogressive, and in the event of our doing anything which had the effect of prejudicing the African population in Rhodesia the British Government could take what steps it wished against this. During the whole of our approach to the problem, Mr Smith had indicated that we had no intention of doing anything which would prejudice the African population, and he pointed out that we would abide by anything we agreed to, but Mr Wilson did not appear to believe us. We asked that we should be given a period of time to prove our *bona fides*.

It was because of this that the idea of a treaty was put forward. Mr Smith pointed out to Mr Heath that he had given his word to Mr Wilson, but that, if it was felt advisable to have an agreement to this in writing, he had no objection to signing the document. During the conversation, however, it appeared that this document was to be a much more formal agreement, and ideas were put forward that the points that had been argued during the various meetings should be incorporated in the agreement. Having indicated that we had no objections to signing a treaty, Conservative representatives contacted Mr Wilson and that night called on him at 10 Downing Street. The next morning we were asked to go to 10 Downing Street and the position of the treaty was then discussed.

The last meeting was no more beneficial than the previous one. We therefore made arrangements to leave on the Monday night and Mr Bottomley came to the airport to see us off. He spoke to me and indicated that Britain would be forced to bring about sanctions if we took the final step, but he said: 'I can assure you that under no circumstances would we use force.' I thanked him for this and indicated to him that, if the British Government felt they had to impose sanctions, all I was asking was that they did not become too vindictive. It is interesting to see what has happened and to know how vindictive these sanctions have become.

On arriving home, Mr Smith got a tumultuous welcome. It was obvious the end of the road had been reached and we had no option but to proceed with what Mr Smith had always told the Rhodesian population

–that he would negotiate to the bitter end, and in the event of this being to no avail we would have to make the final decision. *I then commenced to draw up the 'independence' Constitution and plans were formulated.*

Further letters came. Mr Wilson endeavoured to keep the matter open. I think he had realized when we left that there was no alternative but for us to take Independence. We then had a letter stating that Mr Wilson intended to come out himself. It was a most unprecedented action to take, but was welcome as we felt that something might come of it. Mr Wilson spent his time in Rhodesia speaking to all and sundry, and it was interesting to note that, as far as the Chiefs were concerned, he spent approximately an hour with them but with the African Nationalists the time spent was nearer five hours. It was then that Mr Wilson obviously appreciated that the African Nationalists could not possibly take over the running of this country, and that he made the statement that majority rule could not be achieved immediately and that it was not a question of time and the calendar, but the achievements that would count.

This was really the first public statement reversing the comments of the letter to Dr Mutasa.

Mr Wilson obviously has to try to show that he is always in the right, and therefore we experienced certain theatrical approaches such as the statement he made concerning the hate on the faces of the Ministers at the last meeting at the Prime Minister's house. I was present at this meeting, and the atmosphere, as far as I was concerned, was jovial.

We had again from Mr Wilson the dire consequences that would follow in the event of a declaration of Independence, but I saw no hatred on the faces of

any of the Ministers; I presume, however, that Mr
Wilson thought that it would have a beneficial effect
as far as his case was concerned. This last meeting was
over the question of the Royal Commission. In the after-
noon Mr Wilson had been to see Mr Smith and had suggested the Royal Commission, but it was obvious that his
idea of this Commission was virtually a Constitutional
Conference. We indicated that we would accept the
Royal Commission, provided the Commission's work was
to ascertain whether the people of Rhodesia as a whole
accepted the 1961 Constitution, with the amendments
that we suggested. It was pointed out that it was no
use the Commission putting forward a Constitution that
the Rhodesian Government would not accept. To indicate Mr Smith's attitude supported by the Cabinet, a
communiqué was issued on the Friday and appeared
in Saturday's paper; it was as follows:

'The British Government suggested to the Rhodesian
Government the establishment of a Royal Commission
to settle a Constitution and to determine whether or
not it was acceptable to the people of Rhodesia as a
whole.

'The Rhodesian Government rejected this but proposed instead the appointment of a joint Royal Commission to decide only the question whether or not the
1961 Constitution, with adjustments to make the country
independent, is acceptable to the people of Rhodesia
as a whole.

'The Joint Royal Commission proposed would consist
of a chairman who would be Sir Hugh Beadle, the Chief
Justice of Rhodesia, and two other persons, one to be
appointed by the Rhodesian Government, and one to
be appointed by the British Government.

'The Secretary of State for Commonwealth Relations and the Attorney-General are remaining over for the weekend in order to agree with the Rhodesian Government the adjustments required to the 1961 Constitution.

'The Prime Minister of Great Britain has made it clear that he must secure his Government's approval of the proposals. It is anticipated the British Government's final acceptance or rejection of the proposals can be expected during the coming week.'

From this will be seen that our attitude never varied. On the other hand, everything that Mr Wilson did seemed to make the work of the Commission completely impossible, particularly in suggesting that the Commission should sit and put forward its ideas on how it intended to get the opinion of the Rhodesian people.

Mr Wilson then flew back with his armed bodyguard and retinue, leaving Mr Bottomley and Sir Elwyn Jones and certain advisers to work out an agreement, if possible, and, if no agreement, to establish the points of difference between the two Governments. We had two further meetings on the Saturday and Sunday, but it was obvious that it was completely impossible to get an agreement, as Mr Bottomley persisted in his clichés.

These points of difference were ascertained and were as follows:

'1. At the meeting of British Ministers and the Rhodesian Cabinet on 29th October the two Prime Ministers discussed proposals for an independence Constitution for Rhodesia, which might be put before a Royal Commission to be appointed to ascertain whether such proposals would be acceptable to the people of Rhodesia as a whole. The Prime Minister of Rhodesia maintained that any such proposals must be acceptable to the

Government of Rhodesia and the British Prime Minister accepted the importance of this. The two Prime Ministers agreed that the Commonwealth Secretary, with the Attorney-General and Rhodesian Ministers, should explore the extent of agreement on such proposals which can be reached and should identify the points of disagreement.

2. The results of our discussion are as follows:

(a) ORDINARY CONSTITUTIONAL AMENDMENTS

Rhodesian position

The Rhodesian Government consider that the present provision that the ordinary clauses of the Constitution, other than those specially entrenched, may be amended by a two-thirds majority in the Legislative Assembly should be continued into the independence Constitution unaltered.

British position

The British Ministers suggested that, while this two-thirds provision should be maintained, the B Roll seats in the Legislative Assembly should be increased to provide a "blocking third" for the amendment of these clauses. This proposal is unacceptable to the Rhodesian Ministers.

(b) AMENDMENT OF THE SPECIALLY ENTRENCHED CLAUSES

Rhodesian position

The Rhodesian Ministers regard the present provision for amendment of the specially entrenched clauses by

four racial referenda as unworkable. They would, however, allow this provision to continue into the independence Constitution, provided an acceptable alternative
was introduced for the present arrangements set out in
section 109, whereby in lieu of these referenda a Bill
may be submitted to Her Majesty for assent. The Rhodesian Ministers propose that, in place of this procedure,
a House of twelve Chiefs should be established which
would vote with the Assembly on the third reading of
any Bill seeking to amend the specially entrenched
clauses. The Rhodesian Ministers consider that the
twelve Chiefs, added to the existing fourteen B Roll
members, would provide a predominantly African
"blocking third".

British position

The British Ministers do not regard these proposals
as providing an acceptable substitute for the present
section 109 procedure and point out that the sole constitutional safeguard would be a margin of two votes.
They suggest alternative procedures for the amendment
of specially entrenched clauses, to replace the two alternative procedures in the present Constitution.

The first of these would require that a Bill to amend
a specially entrenched clause should receive a two-thirds
majority in the Legislative Assembly and should then be
submitted to a referendum of the electorate, provided
that the electorate on the B Roll had been increased to
include, say, all adult taxpayers.

The second alternative procedure would be that an
amending Bill should receive a three-quarters majority
in the Legislative Assembly, provision having been made
for an increase in the B Roll seats to provide a "blocking

quarter". Thereafter, before the Bill became law, a fixed time should elapse during which the validity of the Bill could be challenged by any Rhodesian on the grounds (a) that the Bill discriminated or had the effect of discriminating unjustly between the races; (b) that it failed to pay proper respect to the rights and freedoms of the individual. The question of the validity of the Bill would be determined by the appellate division of the High Court of Rhodesia, with an appeal as of right from the decision of that court to the Judicial Committee of the Privy Council.

The Rhodesian Ministers find the first of these alternative procedures (i.e. approval by a two-thirds majority followed by a referendum) unacceptable. They are prepared to consider the second alternative, provided the additional two seats necessary to enlarge the B Roll to a blocking quarter are filled by Chiefs who, on appointment to the Legislature, would cease to receive any Chiefs' subsidies, and provided the reference to the High Court is strictly limited to the question whether the Bill "unjustly discriminates between the races".

The British Ministers consider that the additional two seats on the B Roll should be filled by members elected on the B Roll.

(c) ADDITIONS TO THE SPECIALLY ENTRENCHED CLAUSES

Rhodesian position

The Rhodesian Ministers are not prepared to agree to the further special entrenchment of any clauses in the present Constitution, with the possible single exception referred to below.

British position

The British Ministers suggest the special entrenchment of Chapter III of the Constitution, which is not now specially entrenched in the Constitution. This chapter relates to the delimitation and number of constituences and electoral districts. Without such special entrenchment, it would be possible, by a two-thirds majority, to amend the clauses governing the number of A or B Roll seats.

The Rhodesian Ministers cannot accept the special entrenchment of these clauses. They would, however, agree to the special entrenchment of the provisions governing the total number of B Roll seats, provided a "fade-out" arrangement was introduced into the independence Constitution, under which any reduction in B Roll seats would be dependent on non-Europeans winning A Roll seats. The Rhodesian proposal is that for each A roll seat won by a non-European a B Roll seat should be abolished. This is unacceptable to the British Ministers, who consider that if an arrangement of this kind were to be introduced it should at least provide that two A Roll seats would have to be won by non-Europeans before a B Roll seat was abolished. Additionally, the British Ministers have doubts about this proposal on practical grounds, e.g. the difficulty of definition or of subsequent electoral reversal.

(d) THE FRANCHISE

Rhodesian position

Provided the remaining provisions of the Constitution satisfied their requirements, the Rhodesian Ministers would be willing to extend the franchise on the B Roll to qualified indigenous adult taxpayers.

British position

Provided the remaining provisions of the Constitution satisfied their requirements, and subject to the reasonableness of the proposed qualifications, the British Ministers would accept this.

(e) CONSEQUENTIAL AMENDMENTS

Rhodesian and British Ministers are satisfied that no serious problems are raised by the sequence of amendments, of a consequential nature, which would be necessary to convert the 1961 Constitution into an independence Constitution.

(f) SUBMISSION OF THIS REPORT

It is agreed that this joint report will be submitted by the British and Rhodesian Ministers to their respective Governments.'

I can genuinely say that Mr Smith and the people who accompanied him honestly wished to arrive at a settlement, if possible, but it became obvious from the first meeting that there was no hope whatsoever of arriving at an agreement unless majority rule was accepted, to come into effect in a very short period of time.

It may be asked why we did not accept twelve extra seats on the B Roll. The reply is simply that the 1961 Constitution gave the African the opportunity to become involved in politics but he has not accepted it. The Nationalists had boycotted the Voters' Rolls and the elections, and anyone who knows the mind of the

African will realize that had we given these twelve seats they would have claimed a victory and would never have been satisfied, but merely persisted in their attitude of demanding more and more. The African is not prepared to work for anything, it must be given to him – and this is what the British Government wished to do.

Even if we had agreed to what the British Government offered, it was only a prelude to the unrests that had taken place and would follow, and I think the British Government knew this but had no feeling for the European in this country. We were expendable, and they had to appease not only the Commonwealth but the Afro-Asian bloc as well.

6

A 'Police State'? The Answer

We have been accused of being a Police State and not applying the rule of law. If the allegation was not so serious it would be laughable. For Britain to shout about the rule of law is hypocritical when one knows the action that was taken in Kenya, what is happening in Aden today, and what happened during the Irish Rebellion.

It would be interesting to know how many people the British Government have directly restricted or detained without any pretence of trial. The cry for the rule of law is echoed in the world today, and I can only say that in Rhodesia we respect the rule of law to a far greater extent than many other countries in Africa and elsewhere. A fundamental truth is that the rule of law only operates when there is tranquillity. When there is any chaos it is impossible to apply the rule of law.

Accusations have been made against me of restricting people without trial. Restriction orders have been made against people, but only after full investigations have been made and evidence, which could not be produced in a court of law because of intimidation of witnesses, has been placed before me. To give an example, two saboteurs who admitted using explosives and generally attempting to disrupt the tranquillity of the state were taken before the court but were acquitted on technical grounds. Does any right-thinking person expect me to allow individuals of that type to go free to perpetrate their nefarious acts again, and in all probability bring about the death of some law-abiding citizen? Surely, I would be accused of criminal negligence if I allowed that sort of thing to happen, but because our skins are white the pressure of the Communists and their fellow travellers, backed by many newspapers, accuse the Rhodesian Government of conducting a Police State, and not abiding by the rule of law.

Here, I would like to quote Thomas Jefferson, who declared during the American War of Independence:

'A strict observance of the written law is doubtless one of the high duties of a good citizen, but it is not the highest. The laws of necessity, of self-preservation, of saving our country when in danger are of higher obligation. To lose our country by a scrupulous adherence to written law would be to lose law itself, with life, liberty, property and all those who are enjoying them with us; thus absurdly sacrificing the end for the means.'

It appears that Mr Wilson wishes law and order to break down in this country, so that he can have an excuse to intervene, but the fact that the actions taken by the Government have brought about complete tranquillity has upset his plans and annoyed him intensely. We know that the British authorities have not impeded the Zambian Broadcasting Corporation in the broadcasts of their subversive attacks, which are persisted in with a view to breaking down law and order. We know that the British Government has supplied extra transmitters to be erected near Livingstone because the present Zambian broadcasts are not heard clearly in Rhodesia. If proof is wanted, there it is.

For Mr Wilson to deny that this is the plan is in conflict with the propaganda which is being put out by him in order to undermine the good government in this country. It has been denied that letters from Rhodesia to Britain are censored, but we have evidence to prove that this is the case. Letters from Britain to Rhodesia are being opened in Britain, and not always in a subtle way, as Scotch tape has been used to close them after they have been read. This is the experience of not only myself but of hundreds of people in this country.

Considerable criticism has been levied against us because of our censorship regulations. I notice that Mr Bottomley has criticized me personally for these regulations and, as usual, has endeavoured to put over propaganda detrimental to Rhodesia. It is amazing really, if it was not so serious, because the British papers are much more subject to outside pressures than ours. I will not enlarge on this but informed opinion will understand it precisely.

As far as Rhodesia is concerned, we only have two daily newspapers, both owned by the same group, so that people in Rhodesia are not able to choose any other papers to obtain an objective portrayal of the facts, and these newspapers, in my opinion, appear to be dedicated to the substitution of the present Rhodesian Government by some other Government, and, further, appear intent on helping the British Government in their plans.

The Rhodesian public being what it is must be protected from the vicious propaganda that is being put over by the British Government and which would be

echoed in the local Press. It is the firm determination
of the Rhodesian Government that law and order will
be maintained, and if anything can be done in order
to preserve it we will do it. This includes censorship of
the Press if necessary. The point which is not made clear
to the British public, and elsewhere in the world, is the
fact that any information coming out of Rhodesia is
not censored: Press reports, letters, telegrams and all
other media pass freely over our borders to wherever
they are sent. News which is untrue or slanted can cause
alarm or despondency, or lower the morale of the population, and it must be stopped or we will be playing
right into the hands of the British Government in its
determined intention to break down law and order in
this country.

Some of the news items which have come over the
B.B.C., and other British-controlled media, have been
twisted out of all recognition.

I am satisfied that if any newspaper in Britain issued
propaganda of such a nature that the British Government
did not consider in a moment of crisis that the interests
of the country were being served, appropriate measures
would be taken by that Government. I have no doubt in
my mind that the action taken by the Rhodesian Government is the correct one for peace and tranquillity in
Rhodesia.

During the period of negotiations the frustration that
was being felt in Rhodesia was plain to see. The uncertainty of the position was beginning to tell on the
inhabitants of all colours. Procrastination was the
theme of the British Government, as it knew that the
more uncertain the position was the more likely it
was that the people of this country would become

restive. Could we allow it to continue? The answer was obviously no.

Subsequent events have proved that we were right, and in spite of the outcries of Mr Wilson his actions have had a completely opposite effect to what he had anticipated. He, by his vindictive actions, his punitive sanctions and his mis-statement of facts, has united the Rhodesian population of all colours more than anything else could have done. Evidence comes in daily of the support the Rhodesian Government has from the African. Never have the people been so united as they are in Rhodesia today. All the members of the Rhodesian Front Party are unanimous in their support of the Prime Minister, and numbers of those who have been against the assumption of democratic rights unilaterally have now rallied behind the Prime Minister to a far greater extent than I ever thought possible, with the one determined purpose in their minds that the sanctions will be overcome, that Mr Wilson will be shown that he is fighting a united people, and that we Rhodesians will win in the end.

7

Vindictive Sanctions

Whilst it is not possible to analyse sanctions to any
great extent at this time, I think it would be interesting
to analyse the reasons behind Mr Wilson's action in
imposing the sanctions. He warned us while we were
in London that sanctions would have to be imposed,
one of his reasons being that if he did not the United
Nations would take a hand in the matter and this would
lead to chaos.

It is interesting to see that the British Government
immediately took the matter to the United Nations for
their support. But if we analyse the thinking behind the
imposition of sanctions the conclusion we must arrive
at is that Mr Wilson had received wrong advice. He was
of the opinion that the imposition of sanctions would
divide the people of Rhodesia and there would be a
split in the population. It is easy to realize why he had
this opinion, because he had been receiving advice from
Mr J. B. Johnston, the High Commissioner, and presumably from Sir Humphrey Gibbs.

Mr J. B. Johnston moved in a very secluded circle of
the population, and I think that he had been convinced
by their attitude that the imposition of sanctions would

lead to a complete breakdown of law and order and a split in the country. This was also the opinion of Sir Humphrey, because in discussions I had with him after the 11th November he indicated that he knew that widespread unemployment was imminent, large firms would be closing down, and our actions would cause a breakdown of the economic life in this country. He had received this information from certain individuals, but it is strange that the individuals who told him this expounded an entirely opposite opinion when speaking to members of the Government.

To show how wrongly Mr Wilson was advised, his statement at the Lagos Prime Ministers' Conference bears this out. It will be remembered that he stated that the collapse of the Rhodesian Government would take place within weeks rather than months, and from information that has come to my knowledge he told President Kaunda that the 15th February was 'D' Day. Little did he know what trouble he was storing up for himself by stating a date to the African countries. Those who have had experience with Africans know that if a statement is made it must be carried out, otherwise the person making that statement suffers and the African loses complete respect for him. This is now happening, as I see it.

Another interesting point was the alacrity with which America rallied behind Britain; compare this with the time she took before coming into the First and Second World Wars. She was the first to enter on the side of Britain against Rhodesia. It does make one think, doesn't it? Could it be because of our size?

Sanctions have now been applied to Rhodesia for months in increasing severity so that the world Press

is reporting the Rhodesian situation as a personal ven-
detta by the British Prime Minister against the Rhodesian Government.

What have been the results of sanctions so far?

The main results can be stated as follows:

The first sufferers would be the Africans, whose situation worsens immediately the economy is affected. There
are over a million Africans employed in the great in-
dustries of Rhodesia.

Britain is rapidly losing her markets in Africa, which
are being taken over by her keenest competitors – the
Japanese, the Americans, the West Germans and Italians,
often acting through 'neutral' intermediaries.

Sanctions have failed in the prime objective – to bring
the Rhodesian Government to its knees. After the initial
shock that Britain could employ such methods against
a British Dominion, the Rhodesian Government tackled
the situation. The result has been that regarding oil,
tobacco, and copper, as well as the other commodities,
supplies have been secured and buyers have been found.
Sanctions are condemned because they are ineffective in
every way except the creation of unbelievable hatred
and resentment.

The Association of African States was amazed that
Britain capitulated to their demands to carry on a sanc-
tions war against Rhodesia. British prestige, so high in
Africa until recently, has sunk to an all-time low.

In Salisbury and throughout the country everyone
carries on as before, determined that minor hardships
will not make them surrender and uniting the whole
nation behind the Rhodesian Government in a way that
without sanctions would have been impossible to
achieve.

A situation has been engineered in which the African states will attempt to set a 'dead-line' for the fall of the Rhodesian Government, and when this does not occur they will clamour for force to be used, which means a military invasion of Rhodesia. These nations – for obvious reasons – are not seeking to become the spearhead of military action against Rhodesia themselves, but they calculate that by agitation in the United Nations and in Africa they can either blackmail the British Government into invading Rhodesia on a fabricated excuse that 'law and order' has broken down, or induce a United Nations force to subdue their enemy for them.

Success is not always the best measure in life, but in sanctions it is essential. Sanctions that fail to achieve their objective are disastrous. They cause great bitterness, much economic havoc, and irreparable damage to international relations without gaining one single good result. Sanctions against Rhodesia have so far failed. They are therefore wholly to be condemned.

These actions have had the opposite effect to that envisaged by Mr Wilson. People from various countries in the world, contrary to the Governments of their countries, have realized that the British Government is being vindictive and the support we are receiving is tremendous. Visitors come in every day wishing us luck and advising us not to give in. The 'Friends of Rhodesia' societies that are being formed in various countries are proof of the wide support that people have for us and for our justified legal stand.

The attitude of Rhodesia today is the same as that adopted by Britain after Dunkirk. Then Sir Winston Churchill stated that the British would fight on the beaches and in the streets; we have no beaches, but we will fight in the streets, we will fight in the open, we will do everything in our power to overcome the petty and spiteful attitude adopted by Mr Wilson. Never fear, sanctions will not split Rhodesia; sanctions will not bring us to our knees. We will suffer, but through that suffering we will emerge as a great Rhodesian Nation.

8

Why was Independence Essential to Rhodesia?

Why is Independence so important to us? Why was it necessary for us to take it on the 11th November? Why could we not have continued under the 1961 Constitution which allegedly gave Rhodesia internal self-government without interference from the British Government?

These questions have been asked time and time again. I will endeavour to answer them as best I can.

The British Government had refused to write into the 1961 Constitution the provision that it was precluded from suspending, varying or altering that Constitution by an Act of the British House of Commons, without the consent of the Rhodesian Government. When representatives of all races in Rhodesia negotiated with the British Government for the 1961 Constitution, Rhodesian delegates demanded that a provision to this effect should be inserted in the Constitution, but the British Government refused. It therefore meant that the British Government retained its rights to suspend, revoke or alter our Constitution if it so wished, and proof of this has been furnished by the Passing of the Southern Rhodesia Act of 1965. In the White Paper which was issued prior to the 1961 Constitution being drawn up, it was intimated that there was a convention of non-interference, but it was not included in the Constitution, and therefore one can only conclude that the British Government were not prepared to relinquish the power they considered they had. The Southern Rhodesia Act of 1965 purports to give the British Government the right to suspend, amend, revoke or add to any of the provisions of the 1961 Constitution.

It had become obvious to me that no reliance could be placed upon the British Government not to interfere in our internal affairs, and we have been proved correct in this assessment. Knowing that the word of the British Government could not be trusted, the academic arguments that were put forward to the effect that there existed this convention which precluded the British Government from interfering in our internal affairs did not impress any members of the Rhodesian Government. Having seen what happened in other parts of the African continent in connection with Independence given by the British Government, it became transparently clear that white Rhodesians were expendable in the eyes of the British Government, and therefore it was imperative, as far as we were concerned, that a decision on our Independence was made as soon as possible. Whatever the British Government had said, we knew that it had no intention of giving us our Independence based upon the 1961 Constitution and *their intention was to insist upon majority rule in Rhodesia.* The obvious question which springs to mind is how the Rhodesian Government came to this conclusion.

In the first place, as I have already mentioned, Mr Harold Wilson, as leader of the Labour Party, in 1964 wrote a letter to an African Nationalist named Dr Mutasa in Rhodesia. This letter categorically stated that the Labour Party's policy was that Independence for Rhodesia could only be granted on a basis of majority rule. I think on this evidence it was only reasonable for us to have concluded that this would be the policy of the British Government when Mr Wilson became Prime Minister.

We were not mistaken, and this came to light in the lengthy negotiations which the Rhodesian Government continued with the British Government after Labour's acquisition of power. It was not until a later date, after members of the British Government had talked to the alleged leaders of the African Nationalists, that it dawned upon them that it would be catastrophic to Rhodesia to insist upon majority rule before Independence could be given.

Mr Wilson, therefore, again went back on his word, this time to the African Nationalists, indicating that time and the calendar were not the overwhelming factors; it was the advancement which would count. It was obvious from this change of attitude that Mr Wilson realized that the African in Rhodesia was utterly incapable of taking over the responsibilities of the government of this country.

The Rhodesian Prime Minister, Mr Ian Smith, on the other hand, had always approached the country's Independence from the attitude that the 1961 Constitution was the Constitution which was accepted by all races in the country, and that was the basis upon which Independence should be given, but that any advancement would be based entirely upon merit, irrespective of race or colour.

It also became obvious to me that Britain was losing its position as Head of the Commonwealth, and this was borne out by the agreement at the Commonwealth Prime Ministers' Conference to set up a Commonwealth Secretariat. It was also apparent that with the pressures that were being applied to Britain that country would not have the will or the ability to hold out and that it would hand over the whole of the Rhodesian question to the Secretariat immediately it was constituted. It became perfectly clear that, as far as the British Government was concerned, Rhodesia was not to be the rock upon which the Commonwealth would be wrecked and that, therefore, it could not possibly grant us Independence based upon the 1961 Constitution, because it was of the opinion that *such action would lead to the break-up of the Commonwealth.*

How right we were, as the facts have proved since the 11th November that Britain will do anything to prevent the break-up of the Commonwealth, even to the extent of being insulted in the eyes of the world, and of recognizing bloody revolution and accepting the usurpers of the constitutionally elected Governments as the legal Governments in the African states. *I think it can be accepted that Britain's attitude in bending over backwards to prevent the break-up of the Common-wealth may be the correct decision politically for Britain, but the effect on Rhodesia is catastrophic.*

It also became obvious to us that in power politics, especially world power politics, there is little or no room for sentiment, particularly in a country which is seeking to maintain its status in world power politics as a force to be reckoned with. We had been left in no doubt, through the protracted negotiations, that it would be impossible to obtain Independence based upon anything resembling the 1961 Constitution with the consent of

Britain. Britain intended to wash her hands of the Rhodesian question immediately the Secretariat was established and hand it over to the Commonwealth countries. Mr Wilson had, at various Commonwealth Prime Ministers' Conferences, acceded to the Commonwealth Prime Ministers' insistence that a Constitutional Conference should be held in respect of Rhodesian Independence, and this acceptance by Mr Wilson was again brought to the fore when the Royal Commission was suggested and he intimated that if the Royal Commission did not report unanimously a Constitutional Conference would be held.

Bearing in mind all the points that I have mentioned above, I think any reasonable person must come to the conclusion that the Rhodesian Government, through the determination of the British Government to appease the Commonwealth members and the Afro-Asian Group, had no option but to make the decision it did and to assume its democratic rights on the 11th November 1965.

We have been referred to as 'little frightened men' and having a 'death wish', but this, as I see it, was merely theatrical propaganda in order to convince the British people and the Commonwealth that Mr Wilson had done everything he possibly could to give us Independence but that we had acted completely irresponsibly and recklessly.

A decision to assume one's democratic rights is not taken lightly, and a considerable amount of discussion, heartache and emotional upset ensued prior to the proclamation being signed on the 11th November 1965. Please do not let me imply, in any way, that there was any objection within the Rhodesian Government to the decision. It was unanimous and not forced by the

D

'extremists' in the Rhodesian Government as stated by Mr Bottomley. These allegations again were obviously made with one endeavour and that was to cause a split between the Prime Minister and the rest of the Government. Inferences have been made by Mr Bottomley and others that it was only because of certain elements in the Cabinet that a decision was forced on the Prime Minister. The Prime Minister has, on various occasions, indicated that this was not so, and if any reinforcement is required I say categorically that the decision was unanimous. It was the only way we could avoid the fate which was being planned for us by the British Government, and at the same time only thus could we save Rhodesia from the infiltration of the Communist menace which was seeping through the African continent. Our decision also has been proved to be the wish of the overwhelming majority of the people in Rhodesia, including the Africans.

9

British Government Policy

What is behind British Government policy? Basically it is to back up the United Nations. The Afro-Asian Group, together with the Iron Curtain countries, now dominate the General Assembly and although the veto is still available in the Security Council it seems now to be rarely used.

Rhodesia is the keypoint in the southern portion of Africa and without her fall South Africa and the Portuguese territories are safe. Looking at the map, one sees our position, with Portugal on either side of us and South Africa to the south and west of us. If we were to be overrun by forces hostile to the West, the whole of the southern portion of Africa would ultimately fall. It appears then that the United Nations have embarked on a policy of attrition and by using the Great Powers, notably America, they intend to wear away the resistance of Rhodesia, and once they have overcome this they will move on to South Africa and Portugal.

It is obvious that the time has now arrived when a determined stand must be taken by the nations of Southern Africa to show that under no circumstances would we allow our countries to be picked off individually. Now is the time that we must stand together. The

Zambesi River is the final boundary for African dictator-ship with its Communist supporters.

I remember what Mr Wilson told us when we were in London of the dire consequences of our assuming our democratic rights. He spelt them out and asked us how would we like to have the whole of Beira blockaded by an order of the United Nations. He said that this would be beyond the control of Britain, it would be taken out of her hands by the United Nations and she would be forced, with the others, to blockade Beira to cut off our oil supplies.

He talked of being forced—in fact it was the opposite. He ran to the United Nations because he had to admit that he was being beaten by Rhodesia, and he is like the schoolboy bully who has been thrashed by the small boy whom he picked upon and has called upon his bigger friends to give him the right, with their help, to take vindictive actions against the youngster who has shown so much spirit. He has virtually declared war on us on the pretext that the most tranquil country north of the Limpopo is a threat to world peace. How ridiculous and how juvenile can Britain become? His previous attitude was that the United Nations would force him to do it; he would try to stop it but he doubted if he could. Now we find that Britain has called in the United Nations and seems bent on the use of force against us. If Mr Wilson's move fails and talks break down, in all probability he will then run back to the United Nations and ask them to help him with even more forceful action.

It is obvious that he has been beaten. He has admitted his defeat, and vindictiveness has now come into the whole of his being. We in Rhodesia will win through.

The actions of Britain in boarding ships on the high seas are illegal and constitute a breach of their Marine Code. The resolution at the United Nations has not been passed in terms of its charter. The owners of the oil and the ships have a claim, in my opinion, for large damages, and the officers who committed the acts are chargeable under the penal code.

Yet all this whining and running to the U.N. is really an illustration of what has happened to the Commonwealth since the 'Winds of Change' speech by Mr Macmillan. Everywhere systems based on universal franchise have been overthrown. Take Pakistan as an example. 'One man, one vote' was found not to be workable and a Commission was set up to go into the position. The recommendations were that the voting should be on a qualitative basis. The conclusion arrived at in Pakistan is that the illiterate are unable to assess the value of the candidates and are subject to intimidation and improper persuasion. The report indicates that while the Commission was not prepared to lay down what the qualifications would be, it suggested that a committee should ascertain these qualifications. Fundamentally, education must be the first qualification for the vote, but alternative qualifications such as income and property could be usefully employed. Those who own property know that they have a stake in the country and they tend to work harder for the benefit of that country; those who do not are not worried because they can always leave the country and start life anew. In Pakistan it has been proved that orderly government demands an educated electorate.

Yet even with examples like this the attitude of Britain in the granting of a Constitution is governed by expediency, without consideration being given to the consequences which may follow. Independence is given without any guarantee of any sort of democracy. I have read the Mauritius Constitutional Conference report, and whereas the British Government have been adamant with us that there should be a referendum of all the adults in Rhodesia to see whether the people as a whole would accept the Constitution this same insistence is not accepted by the British Government as far as Mauritius is concerned. It is obvious that the reason for this change of face is that the British Government appreciates that the majority in Mauritius, in all probability, do not want Independence, and if a referendum was held the results would be against Independence. To get over this difficulty, the Constitution is to be ratified by an ordinary vote – not even a two-thirds majority – of the Members of Parliament, who will themselves be elected at an election held under the terms of the new Constitution! There was no such suggestion to us. When one sees what happened in Pakistan, when it was found that the uneducated were unable to contribute to the election of candidates in a responsible manner, it is hard to understand why the British insist upon this referendum. Its only purpose must be to try to hand over the Government of Rhodesia to an uneducated, unqualified African population to the detriment of the Europeans, the Africans themselves and the future stability and prosperity of the country.

The British attitude is one of appeasement, without any thought of the future of this part of the world. As long as what Britain does is for her own good, that is all that counts; the justice of the case or the history of good and stable government in this country counts little with her. By contrast, we in Rhodesia are concerned with building a great future for all our people, and to this end we want the African to play his full part.

Already Africans can form their own political parties and fight the elections provided they work within the Constitution. I personally have had interviews with certain Africans who wished to start a new political party and I made it quite clear that, as far as the Government was concerned, we welcomed its formation provided it acted constitutionally.

The attitude of the Africans, however, is extremely peculiar. There is no question of the democratic appointment of the leaders; they do not hold a convention or meeting to appoint them. The leaders appoint themselves and then go out to collect their members. At no time in Rhodesia have any of the African Nationalist parties had a democratic vote for the appointment of any of their leaders. The African approach seems to be one of personal power. We had one interesting example of this in a statement of one of our Members of Parliament. When he was asked, by one of the British visitors who came to Rhodesia, why they were not prepared to work to gain parliamentary experience so that by the time they did come into power they would know how to govern, his reply was simply: 'We wish to be in power now – we can learn how to administer Government once we are in power.' Throughout Africa there has been the dangerous example of ministerial corruption; money has been salted away in different countries in the personal accounts of Ministers, bribes have been taken, and favours given. This has been the result of an immature and inexperienced government.

Yet the brickbats are reserved not for the corrupt but for us, the Government of this country. We are made out to be a minority group, grinding down the African. We were democratically elected by all registered voters in the country and the Prime Minister was appointed by the party. All persons have been elected, and have not seized power.

Propaganda through the British Government has also endeavoured to show that the reason we assumed our democratic rights was in order to control the African. If analysis of what has happened since the 11th November is made, it will be noticed that we have done nothing which is contrary to the position as it was prior to the 11th November. The Constitution has been changed, but only in respect of the clauses which allowed Britain to have a certain say in respect of our affairs.

It will be remembered that the 1961 Constitution was negotiated by all races and parties and the conclusions were arrived at by the consent of all except the Dominion Party. This Constitution was then accepted by the electorate of Rhodesia by approximately a two-thirds majority, and was put into force as the wish of the country. The African Nationalists, however, when confronted by their extremist wing, went back on what they had agreed to and boycotted the elections, and that is the reason why there are no more Africans on the Voters' Roll. The numbers who could get on if they weren't intimidated by the Nationalists are far in excess of the numbers that are there at the moment. Had the Nationalists co-operated in the Constitution, they would obviously have been able to put forward their grievances in the proper constitutional manner. Had they co-operated Rhodesia would have gone from strength to strength.

The attitude, however, is so typical. The African

Nationalist is not prepared to work for anything. He thinks that Britain will give him everything he wants provided he shouts sufficiently. If he boycotts something, then the European will give in. Unfortunately for the Rhodesian extremist, he has now been faced with people who have lived in this country all their lives, people who have built up the country to what it is, people who do not intend to be scared, as the Europeans to the north of us were. When the Congo crisis took place we looked after thousands of Belgians who fled in panic from the Congo, and this caused our first riot, as the African in Rhodesia considered that the European was on the run; he had come out of the Congo, he was fleeing from the African, and therefore the African Nationalists tried their riots in Rhodesia to see whether the European would start running from Rhodesia as well. They found out that this was not the attitude of the Rhodesian European; he was here to stay.

This was the first lesson that the African Nationalists in this country learnt, that they could not intimidate the Rhodesians, but the Rhodesians, because of their acceptance of the 1961 Constitution, were quite prepared to co-operate with the Africans and work for the benefit of the country as a whole and for all the races within it. This fact does not appear to have been accepted by Britain; it appears to have been purposely overlooked. With the successes that the British have had with the countries to the north of us, where they have been able to insist and virtually bulldoze the Europeans to accept the requirements of the Africans it was thought that they could do the same here, and this is what they have been endeavouring to do. Why the sanctions? Why the mandatory rights to use force on the high seas? The answer is because they have been frustrated in their intentions. They thought they could overcome the European in Rhodesia with ease, but they have found out that they cannot.

Another criticism that we are faced with is that we do not give the African the opportunity to improve himself. People do not seem to realize that the Civil Service, for example, is completely multi-racial. People are appointed to it on ability and not because of their colour.

In May 1964 there were 6,413 Africans employed in the Rhodesian Public Service, and that figure did not include approximately 11,000 office orderlies, drivers and other junior division officers. In the police and the army we have thousands of Africans. These people are able to work their way right up to the top. There is no question of getting promotion on colour, so that everybody has an opportunity to get as far as his merit allows.

In the railways at the beginning of March 1965 there were 807 Africans in the National Industrial Council grades. Of these, 140 are employed as locomotive firemen and 45 of them as firemen qualified to sit examinations for promotion as locomotive drivers. Here again it is not a question of race or colour, it is a question of ability and aptitude. It goes through the whole of our economic structure. We have Africans who earn up to £6,000 a year in their own businesses, and in commerce and industry there are many highly paid Africans in positions which were originally taken by Europeans.

There is no truth in the allegation that we wish to keep the African down and are not prepared to allow him to improve. We have done everything in our power to improve the African, because we realize that the races must work together or we all shall be courting trouble. The average employed African is a happy man; a law-abiding individual unconcerned with politics of the type that the Nationalists indulge in. I am certain that the manner in which we are working together will enable us to forge ahead in a country where everybody is entitled to advance on grounds of ability, and where there will be no discrimination on grounds of colour.

The policy of this Government is not to force integration. If people wish to integrate, then provisions have been made for them to do so. Since this Government came into power it has created in Gwelo, my home town, a multi-racial area. There are also such areas in Bulawayo and Salisbury.

Automatic segregation takes place everywhere, even in Britain, in spite of legislation which prohibits discrimination. Whilst a multi-racial state can be created, and is being created, in Rhodesia, it can only be done on a voluntary basis and not by legislation. Legislation creates hatred, whereas voluntary mixing of the races can create goodwill.

Our education provisions are expanding apace. There are over 200 Africans in our university taking various degrees, and we are extending the secondary education as fast as our finances will allow. One must appreciate, however, that at present there are vacancies in secondary schools because there are not enough Africans qualifying to enter those schools. This may come as a revelation to people who are always arguing that we are not trying to educate the African. In spite of the fact that the schools are not fully occupied, it is intended to proceed further with the building of new secondary schools so that the opportunity will be there all the time for the furtherance of the education of the African.

I think there is a fundamental difference which needs to be discussed between the outlook of the British and Rhodesian Governments about education. The British think that a person must be educated for political ends, for the purpose of the vote. The economic position of the country appears to be overlooked completely. We have had suggestions from the British Government that they would spend money, but we have never had any really practical demonstration of it. It has always been words, never deeds. We did have a visit from a Minister to see whether they could help us in the furtherance of education, but when we put forward the point that we would be prepared to accept anything that was offered for the furtherance of education, provided there would also be loans or grants of money for the economic advancement of the country, the British seemed to shy off; the two did not appear to go together.

We seem unable to get it into the minds of the British politicians that it is no use educating hundreds of Africans if there is no suitable work for them – such a situation creates a breeding ground for subversion and Communism. If one educates a person, one must give him the opportunity to make a living. Idle hands are the cause of trouble, and therefore it is very necessary for us to exploit the economic potential of the country in order that opportunities for work may be given to all those people who are educated, so that they may provide for their families and live a happy life in this country. It is a peculiar thing that the African who considers himself educated is not prepared to accept employment of a manual nature.

Politics is not the be all and end all of existence. Politics do play a part in the progress of the country, but the Government's main job is the welfare of the people. We have endeavoured, particularly through our efforts in agriculture, to expand the openings for employment. We are now encouraging tenant farming, and provide loans to individuals to enable them to increase their food production. We have also endeavoured to have more concentrated agricultural production in the irrigation areas, and to teach the Tribal Trust African modern methods of farming.

We have been accused of allocating land to the African which is useless compared with the land occupied by the European. This is not true. The difference has been the approach to agricultural production. The European has farmed the land properly, the African much less so. There are examples of European farms of exactly the same soil and climate, adjacent to the African Tribal Trust area, which produce between twenty and thirty bags of maize per acre, whereas over the border the Africans are getting returns of approximately three bags per acre.

When, as has happened in the Chiweshe Reserve, Europeans have helped the African in the farming of his land, he has improved his yield to reach that of the European. It is all a matter of education, and we are continuing to try to enable the African to reach a standard of living sufficient to create a demand for consumer goods. This will be the take-off point for the whole economy of a country in which subsistence living can only be a burden on the community.

Our education efforts can be divided into the academic and vocational. The academic potential in a country of this size is limited, but the need for vocational training is vast. It is therefore desirable, as I see it, for the first

steps to be that the majority be given vocational training
to equip them for life.

All those plans for education, farming improvements,
and political advancement are expensive and yet we
are prepared to pay the price. Rhodesia is not the wicked
nation it is painted. If it were, then why do half a million
alien Africans, including families, come from the northern countries to work in Rhodesia? It is because the
conditions are so much more pleasant and the economic
situation so much better. If we were such a bad country,
would not these people remain in their own nations
where they have 'freedom' and 'independence'? These
good conditions which prevail in Rhodesia cannot continue if the sanctions go on. We may have to get rid of
all these alien Africans and send them back to the north,
which will not improve the economic position of the
northern territories.

I am perfectly satisfied that the future of the African
in Rhodesia is bright as long as the European remains.
If the European was to leave because of the attitude of
the British Government, then the lot of the African
would be disastrous. Many would starve and the others
would go back to the days of the marauders and the
cattle rustlers. Tribal enmity would return with renewed
force and there would be strife and warfare. Without
the European here, the Africans cannot advance. There
are many Africans who appreciate this, and that is why
we have had such peace and tranquillity since the 11th
November. The position is quieter today than it has
been for the past seven years. The Africans realize, seeing
the graft and bad Government that has continued in
the northern territories ruled by their own people, that
they are much better off in Rhodesia with a European

Government. They naturally demand opportunities, and they will be given the chance, as they always have had in this country, to better themselves and to proceed to acquire wealth, property and the means to bring up their children in the manner they would wish. The races can work together in co-operation in this country, to create a great nation.

Life in Rhodesia is pleasant for all. It has been alleged that it is pleasant because of the differing standards of living between the Europeans and the Africans. These differences are becoming less marked as the African advances. The British seem to want us to lower the European standards to those of the African, so that we could get a unified territory on a pauper basis. But we cannot allow standards to drop – we cannot allow individuals to have short-cuts to qualifications – they must go through the exams as everybody else has to, and they must qualify in the proper manner. We want to raise the standards of all, not debase those of the advanced.

The climate in this country is beautiful; the sunshine and the people make it such a wonderful place to live in. I have never heard of anyone who has been out here not considering it to be a country worth living in. Only fellow travellers object because they feel that, as the Europeans and Africans are not living socially integrated, the nation is unworthy. What a curious attitude! Everywhere in the world people have differing standards of living, and everywhere people are entitled to choose their company, their friends, and companions.

In Rhodesia today discrimination is being overcome with multi-racial hotels and multi-racial cinemas, and now it is generally true that the Africans are entitled to most of the conveniences the Europeans have. They have, of course, their own areas into which the Europeans cannot go, and they would not want them there. The Africans are a very proud race and they do not wish for complete integration. They are satisfied with some separation but realize that we must work together for this country.

The increase of industrial production and basic mineral extraction will make this a better country to live in. But we must be left alone. We will sort out our own troubles, and find an answer which will not be to the detriment of any race but for the betterment of the whole country and of all the races who occupy it.

Give us five years to test the genuineness of the European. Give us an opportunity to work out a Constitution acceptable to all. It is necessary for us to have investigations into what the Constitution should be. Western democracy, as practised in Britain, has failed in Africa – give us a chance to make freedom work.

I believe that we can adopt a Constitution to protect the rights of the different races so that, regardless of who is in power, those rights will always be protected.

If our skins were black, we would have our Independence – the British could not have cared less; but because we are white they feel they have a duty to impose upon us a system which would bring about the collapse of the economy and the collapse of the country as a whole. When, oh when, will they see sense? When will they realize that their policy is so completely wrong? When will they realize that for the benefit of human beings, irrespective of colour, they should stop interfering with things they know nothing about?

10

Rhodesia of Tomorrow

Whilst we are in the midst of the battle considerable thought is being given to the pattern of Rhodesia of tomorrow. It is appreciated by all who live in this country that all races must live in harmony for the benefit of the country and themselves, with the more 'well-to-do' members of the population helping those who are not so 'well-to-do'. We have to proceed with the education of the people, and this we are doing to the full commensurate with the finances available. The economic potential of the country must be expanded to the full to the benefit of all persons here.

The demand for education by Africans has risen phenomenally since the war. Today they are working in many places to open 'community' schools, and there is great pressure for local councils to run schools in the Tribal Trust Lands and Purchase Areas. This is an encouraging sign that the people are growing in responsibility and self-reliance.

The heavy demand has, however, led Africans to become impatient, and complaints are often heard that the Government is not doing as much as it could. These complaints may seem reasonable to one not knowing the facts or who has not taken the trouble to compare our achievements with those of other African countries. But our record is nevertheless a proud one, and continuing strenuous efforts are being made to provide Africans with the schooling they need.

Whilst authoritative figures are not always available from other countries, the following information provided by Unesco is revealing. Nearly 45 per cent of the world's population is completely illiterate. In 57 per cent of the countries less than half the school-age population is in school. Literacy in North and Western Europe is the highest – over 98 per cent. Africa and India have between 10 per cent and 15 per cent. In Rhodesia the literacy rate for Africans is approximately 30 per cent.

In regard to the proportion of pupils in school, accurate figures are difficult to obtain for other countries in Africa, but indications are that Rhodesia has the highest proportion in school. Some of our severest critics amongst African countries have the lowest proportion. Rhodesia's achievements in African education have been virtually without assistance from external sources. Finance and staff are the two main barriers to more rapid educational expansion in Rhodesia.

Of the 4,080,000 Rhodesian Africans today, half are under the age of seventeen. This means that there is one adult per child – in England there are three, and they are more productive than the average worker here.

The European taxpayer provides the great bulk of the revenue – estimated at over 98 per cent (1964) of the individual and company income taxes – and probably the larger proportion of the indirect taxes. African school fees from urban Government schools in 1965 totalled £231,000, whilst European fees collected amounted to

£935,000 – over four times as much. Africans in the rural areas, however, collectively pay considerable amounts in fees towards the missions and churches.

There was a belief amongst Africans that when their personal tax was raised to £2 per annum some years ago, this would enable the Government to provide for all their educational needs. In fact, this particular revenue amounted to only a small proportion of that spent on African education. This tax has now been modified and in some districts the Local Government Councils collect it for development purposes. The doubling of this tax was designed to provide every child with the first segment of primary education— from Sub A to Standard 3 – and this has been fulfilled. We have now progressed far beyond that stage and gone a long way towards meeting the demand for primary education for all. It is not generally realized that when the Government sanctions a new Sub A class it commits itself financially to completing the segment. If it approves a Standard 4 it must also approve Standards 5 and 6 as well. For this reason the Government is not able to approve applications for additional segments without careful consideration of the resources available.

It appears that Rhodesia has at last caught up with the demand for entry into the primary schools. For the past two years there has actually been a drop in intake. It is estimated that 95 per cent of eligible children in the lower primary group are in schools. The country can now apply itself more to the upper primary and the secondary sectors.

The amount spent on African education in 1965 was £6·45 million. In 1949 it was just over half a million pounds, and in 1956 it was under £3 million. The enrolment of African pupils has doubled over the past ten years; and this year there are approximately 643,000 pupils in school. The enrolment in secondary schools has increased sixfold over the same period.

The wisdom of turning out large numbers of well educated people for whom jobs may not be available has been questioned – unemployment could be a serious problem, not only in Rhodesia but in many independent countries in Africa. The educational output ought obviously to be in gear with the industrial development of Rhodesia.

Critics sometimes point out that about ten times as much is spent for each European child. There are adequate reasons for this. In the first place, of the 643,000 pupils in African schools, over 95 per cent are in primary schools, which cost a fraction of secondary schools to build and run. In the second place, European pupils receive no better schooling than they would expect anywhere else, and their parents are the main taxpayers who also pay for the bulk of African education. In the third place, Africans have shown interest in education only during the past two or three decades, and in the light of this the expansion has been truly phenomenal. In the fourth place, in order to equalize African with European education it would cost twice Rhodesia's entire budget. It should also be borne in mind that nine-tenths of Africans' schooling is in the rural areas, where they build their own schools with the assistance of the missions.

Lowering the standards (which have taken generations to achieve) in order to spend more on African education would doubtless cause many Europeans to emigrate, with a resultant fall in revenue; and would also discourage expatriate teachers from coming to Rhodesia. Raising the standards of African education is the aim, and it calls for more expatriate staff – already extremely difficult to recruit. Of the 666 qualified secondary teachers in African education today, about 130 are Africans.

It is the enterprise of the European population (with, of course, the help of largely unskilled labour) that has been responsible for developing the country's natural resources, building its towns, factories, communications system, its administration, and various institutions which in turn provide employment. It should not be necessary to draw attention to these axioms, but in today's heady climate of opinion people too easily overlook the phenomenal achievements brought about – let it be honestly acknowledged – by the Europeans, without whom the country would fall back into an abyss. The dangers of collapse are far greater in a country like Rhodesia, with a complex economy and developed administration, than they are in comparatively undeveloped countries in Africa to the north.

It is said by some critics that the grading of Standard 6 pupils is carefully designed to keep Africans out of the secondary schools. This is, of course, nonsense. The fact is that the grading has been designed to ensure the maximum benefit from secondary schooling, for it has been found that only students having first-grade and second-grade passes are capable of benefiting academically from formal secondary education. Investigations conducted by staff of the University College of Rhodesia have confirmed this and shown the correlation between Standard 6 passes and success in secondary education.

In a community school which takes in these lower grades, only ten pupils out of over 200 passed their Junior Certificate. There is hardly wastage of promising talent through grades 3, 4 and 5 students not being able to continue with formal education. Engineers, scientists and administrators are unlikely to come from such lower-grade students. Normally, approximately 25 per cent of students are expected to obtain grades 1 and 2 passes. This roughly corresponds with the rate of progression to secondary schools elsewhere.

The main clamour today appears to be for secondary education. This is a good deal more expensive, and staff are at a premium; but the places available are roughly equal to the number of students qualifying to enter. Of the 27,513 pupils sitting for Standard 6 in 1965, 7,009 obtained grades 1 and 2 passes, representing 25 per cent. Of these latter, 6,059 went to secondary schools. In 1965, 768 went on to lower teacher training and industrial courses, and were drawn from grades 1, 2 and 3 passes. Of the remaining small number, about 10 per cent were girls who were not allowed by their parents to continue. In 1956 there were 1,758 secondary pupils in the schools. By 1965 the figure increased to 11,500 (plus a like number studying by correspondence). This surely demolishes the argument that secondary education is being held back.

It is not normal anywhere in the world for the whole school population to expect secondary education. Twenty-three million adults in the United States of America have less than eight years of schooling – roughly the equivalent of Standard 6. (In Britain only 34 per cent continue their schooling beyond the age of 15.) Those having grades lower than 1 and 2 in Standard 6 must accommodate themselves to semi-skilled work. Trade schools could play a more useful part. The demand by Africans for this type of training tended to be disappointingly low, but there is now evidence of renewed interest. Plans are in hand to provide more facilities for technical and vocational training.

This country long ago decided on a broad-based education, giving more opportunity for the bulk of the population to obtain primary education. Most other countries in Africa chose rather to educate a few, as highly as possible. For this reason, countries like Kenya, Uganda, and Tanzania have a larger number of G.C.E. 'A' level passes than Rhodesia, but Rhodesia has a far higher percentage in school, and thus will now rapidly overtake those countries in the secondary sphere.

Correspondence courses have been planned to step up still further the campaign for secondary education. Under this scheme twenty or more students may gather under a responsible organizer, with a reduction in the normal fees. There are, of course, night schools in various centres, and adult education is also being actively pressed. In 1965 there were approximately 12,000 African students taking secondary courses with the correspondence colleges. This gives, with those in the schools, about 24,000 who are in the secondary sector.

It is necessary to state here that special assistance has been given to Africans' education. The external J.C. and Standard 6 examinations were introduced for them; and though Africans may think these a money-making concern, the fact remains that the costs of running these examinations are greater than the fees collected from students. Numbers of bursaries are given each year.

All African students at our multi-racial university are eligible for Government support. In addition, certain qualified African students are eligible for Government support in universities elsewhere. If these grants, loans or bursaries were to be issued on a non-racial basis, purely on academic standards, none of these African students at the university would have qualified for them. (This position has recently changed, since one African student has qualified by his own merit.)

In the pass lists for the H.S.C. 1963 the top seventy pupils were Europeans. As far as sixth-form places are concerned, there are at present more available than there are African students offering themselves. The fourth-form passes have almost doubled over the past year, however, and consideration is being given to expansion for sixth-form students. Of the 863 students sitting the Cambridge Overseas Examinations in 1965, 170 obtained first-division passes, 18 per cent entered the lower sixth, others entered T1 and T2 courses, took scholarships, or went into industry.

Concerning technical education, we have seen Luveve College, in Bulawayo, closing because of poor support. Because of this Luveve became a secondary school in January 1965. Africans complained that the standard of entry for Luveve Technical College was too high, but this was the same for colleges of this status in Britain. Meanwhile, technical colleges in Rhodesia are non-racial, and numbers of Africans already attend these institutions.

There is nationally a need for more industrial schools, but the demand for agricultural, building and carpentry courses by Africans has, until recently, tended to fall, academic courses having a greater appeal. Many Africans are not attracted to courses involving manual work. Chibero Agricultural College, built at high cost, had been very poorly supported until 1965, despite bursaries offered to every student and the promise of well-paid jobs. Today, however, the college is full for the first time.

It has always been our opinion that certain sections of the population continued to look over their shoulders to a mythical godmother 6,000 miles away, hoping that she would bring about some permanent solution to the problem, and while she existed they were not prepared to co-operate with the rest of the population of Rhodesia. Once the apron strings were cut, we knew that this section would realize that they had only themselves to fall back on and would be more ready to co-operate with the other sections of the population. It has always been our contention that the people of Rhodesia would sort out their own difficulties without any outside interference. This will happen. The Chiefs, who have been referred to as paid lackeys of the Rhodesian Government, are leaders of the people in the Tribal Trust Land and their advice will always be sought. Opportunities will be given for the advancement of all people; co-operation will be sought from all races. The Constitution which may not be based upon the Westminster type of Government, will have to be worked out, and I am satisfied that this will be done by the people of Rhodesia.

Rhodesia is a land of opportunity and of wealth, and it is obvious that, given a chance to exploit these opportunities and the wealth that is in the land, she can, under the leadership of Mr Ian Douglas Smith, blossom forth as a united nation to play her part in this world today, more particularly in stopping the spread of Communism throughout the African continent, and in raising the standard of life for all her citizens in freedom and in peace.

Index